Making Partnerships Work

John L. Mariotti

- Fast track route to getting the most from partnerships

- Covers the key areas of partnering, from understanding the different reasons for partnerships and alliances to initiating and succeeding with partnering

- Examples and lessons from some of the world's most successful businesses, including Canon, Sony, Procter & Gamble, Manco, Henkel, Wal*Mart and Dell, and ideas from the smartest thinkers, including Gary Hamel, Yves Doz, Jordan Lewis, Doug McGregor, Abraham Maslow, Stephen Dent, and Sam Walton

- Includes a glossary of key concepts and a comprehensive resources guide

OPERATIONS

06.10

>>EXPRESS EXEC.COM<<
essential management thinking at your fingertips

Copyright © Capstone Publishing 2002

The right of John L. Mariotti to be identified as the author of this work has been asserted in accordance with the Copyright, Designs and Patents Act 1988

First published 2002 by
Capstone Publishing (a Wiley company)
8 Newtec Place
Magdalen Road
Oxford OX4 1RE
United Kingdom
http://www.capstoneideas.com

All rights reserved. Except for the quotation of short passages for the purposes of criticism and review, no part of this publication may be reproduced, stored in a retrieval system, or transmitted, in any form or by any means, electronic, mechanical, photocopying, recording or otherwise, without the prior permission of the publisher.

CIP catalogue records for this book are available from the British Library and the US Library of Congress

ISBN 1-84112-223-8

Printed and bound in Great Britain

This book is printed on acid-free paper

> Substantial discounts on bulk quantities of Capstone books are available to corporations, professional associations and other organizations. Please contact Capstone for more details on +44 (0)1865 798 623 or (fax) +44 (0)1865 240 941 or (e-mail) info@wiley-capstone.co.uk

Contents

Introduction to ExpressExec v

06.10.01	Introduction	1
06.10.02	Definition of Terms	5
06.10.03	Evolution	13
06.10.04	The E-Dimension	27
06.10.05	The Global Dimension	39
06.10.06	The State of the Art	53
06.10.07	In Practice	73
06.10.08	Key Concepts and Thinkers	91
06.10.09	Resources	109
06.10.10	Ten Steps to Making It Work	117

Frequently Asked Questions (FAQs) 129
Index 131

Introduction to ExpressExec

ExpressExec is 3 million words of the latest management thinking compiled into 10 modules. Each module contains 10 individual titles forming a comprehensive resource of current business practice written by leading practitioners in their field. From brand management to balanced scorecard, ExpressExec enables you to grasp the key concepts behind each subject and implement the theory immediately. Each of the 100 titles is available in print and electronic formats.

Through the ExpressExec.com Website you will discover that you can access the complete resource in a number of ways:

» printed books or e-books;
» e-content – PDF or XML (for licensed syndication) adding value to an intranet or Internet site;
» a corporate e-learning/knowledge management solution providing a cost-effective platform for developing skills and sharing knowledge within an organization;
» bespoke delivery – tailored solutions to solve your need.

Why not visit www.expressexec.com and register for free key management briefings, a monthly newsletter and interactive skills checklists. Share your ideas about ExpressExec and your thoughts about business today.

Please contact elound@wiley-capstone.co.uk for more information.

Introduction

The first chapter explains why partnerships and alliances are so essential to managers in the twenty-first century.

The simple fact is that today's supercharged, turbulent, technology-rich, global business environment is so complex that no one can be good enough at everything. Nor should they even try. No company and no individual can be really good at more than a core set of competencies, and these are constantly evolving. The conclusion that follows from this premise is that everyone – individually and organizationally – needs partners to complement what it is they have decided to be good at.

If you will accept for the moment that everyone needs partners, and that nearly everyone has partners already, then the ability to make partnerships work becomes one of the critical core competencies of the twenty-first century. Many of the existing partnerships are flawed; some are broken; others are just bad clichés. But the ones that are really working are incredibly powerful.

The power of these highly functioning partnerships is an even stronger reason that making partnerships work is imperative for success in the current and future business environment. If these points are not sufficient to convince you of that fact, I want to add a few more.

> "Goodbye mergers and acquisitions. In a global market tied together by the Internet, corporate partnerships and alliances are proving a more productive way to keep companies growing."
> *"Partner or Perish," FORBES.COM, Best of The Web,*
> *May 21, 2001*

In the current global business competition, whoever chooses and keeps the best partners will win. The best suppliers; the best customers; the best employees; the best special advisers and consultants; the best joint-venture partners, all working in concert will make the best competitive enterprise. The weak may band together, but even a large coalition of second-rate performers cannot beat a collaborative alliance of the best.

The evidence is all around us. The behemoths of the past, with their vertically integrated businesses, are disintegrating – and I chose that word purposely. Consider General Motors and Ford. Both have divested their captive parts divisions, Delphi and Visteon. Consider AT&T and Lucent (the formerly mighty "Ma Bell"). Each of them is spinning off parts faster than a disintegrating turbine engine. Still others, such as Kodak and Xerox, are struggling to find a corporate core around which to reconfigure.

> "Equally novel are the demands partnerships and alliances make on managing a business and its relationships. Executives are used to command ... But in a partnership one cannot command. One can only gain trust."
>
> *Peter Drucker*

These are the companies that brutalized suppliers, treated customers with haughty disdain, and developed, in their own unions, their worst adversaries. Chrysler, which found and used the power of partnerships in the 1990s, has been dismantled from the top down, and is being recast in the shadow of its owner, Daimler-Benz. The first initiative of DaimlerChrysler when in trouble was to strong-arm suppliers for money, and cut anyone who spoke out in honest dissent.

Companies like Toyota and Honda may be tough, but they are tightly linked to a network of partners. Cisco, in spite of its temporary difficulties, has a similar network of partners. Dell reinvented the supply chain and how computers are built, based on a network of partners surrounding its plants.

But partnerships that work are not all touchy-feely, soft-hearted deals. There is a valuable and necessary tension between the soft and hard sides. The soft side has to do with the human issues of trust and the relationship part of the partnership. The hard side has to do with the fact that partnerships must consistently deliver something of value for both/all partners. This requires clear understandings, specific stated expectations, measurable goals, detailed commitments, vigilant follow-up, and single-mindedness of purpose – nothing less.

There is no room in a partnership for types who talk a good game, but who don't get done what they said they would do. This goes for all partnerships whether they are with customers, suppliers, joint venture partners, or employees. Partnerships are all about promises and commitments – to be kept – by both partners.

As the last death knell sounds for employee loyalty, the only new social contract that makes any sense to people in today's volatile employment world is that of a partnership – in some form. In fact, partnerships provide a solid foundation for loyalty that is hard to find in business these days. Obviously, making partnerships work is both a critical skill and a powerful strategy. In the future, it will only grow in importance. That is why the material that follows is so important.

Remember: no one can be good enough at everything, and whoever chooses and keeps the best partners will win. That's why making partnerships work is so important. Now let's get on with the why and how.

> "In 2000 the number of alliances exploded to more than 10,200. According to consultants, more than 80% of top executives consider strategic alliances to be a prime vehicle for future growth. They also expect alliances to account for 25% of their company's market value within 5 years."
>
> *Matthew Schifrin (ed.), FORBES.COM, Best of The Web,*
> *May 21, 2001*

Definition of Terms

This chapter defines many of the most commonly used forms of partnerships, the reasons for forming them, and illustrates some common applications for partnerships.

PARTNERSHIPS

Before we go any further, let me define what I mean by a "partnership."

> A partnership is an interdependent relationship between people and/or organizations in which they work together to achieve some mutual goals, and in which each invests resources and takes risks in return for rewards.

Many other people have defined partnerships in different ways, and I will tell you more about those as we move through the book. Because there are so many different kinds of relationships that are called partnerships, it is not surprising to find many definitions.

BASIC TYPES OF PARTNERSHIPS

There are four fundamental kinds of partnerships; these are classed as partnerships with:

» Customers
» Suppliers
» Employees and associates
» Special partners – professional or personal.

These kinds of partnerships include "strategic alliances," which can be loosely classified as a special partnership. But strategic alliances are a breed unto themselves, and worthy of special consideration, especially when they are alliances between competitors.

There is actually a fifth type of "partnership" but it is between people and technology. Technology can't make partnerships successful, but the lack of it can make them less successful and even cause them to fail. In today's knowledge- and information-intensive global business environment, technology and its potential for helping people may be a new form of partnership – and one that must work if the business is to maximize its success!

CATEGORIES OF PARTNERSHIPS

For reasons of simplicity I have chosen the six categories listed below. Since each partnership is unique, there are an infinite number of unique categories and reasons for partnerships. Six basic categories may be too few, but there are certainly less than ten fundamental categories, and the more categories I defined, the more they began to overlap. These can be thought of as the "why" in "why form partnerships?"

- » Marketing and/or customer access
- » Technology and/or proprietary know-how
- » Capacity and/or physical resources
- » Skills and/or talent – human resources
- » Financial and/or economic resources
- » Special situations.

FORMS OF PARTNERSHIPS, ALLIANCE, OR JOINT INVOLVEMENT

Most people agree that partnerships and alliances might be classed in a few distinct ways:

- » Partnerships – Close-knit working relationships between a variety of partners – people, organizations, and companies – pursuing common goals in an interdependent manner, but without necessarily sharing (legal) ownership.
- » Alliances – Less tightly bound arrangements between companies or organizations to achieve strategic or tactical goals based on complementary capabilities, but not shared ownership.
- » Joint ventures – Legal agreements based on shared commitments and shared rewards, and often, with shared ownership.
- » Mergers and acquisitions – Transactions in which companies, or parts thereof, are bought or sold to reform the participants' combination of capabilities, markets served, and financial structure.
- » Transactional partnerships – Usually arm's-length or buy–sell relationships based on contractual agreements, and not usually indicative of a high level of trust, commonality of goals, or interdependence outside of the specific transaction involved. (Not really much of a "partnership.")

ALLIANCES

Noted author and partnership authority Jordan Lewis describes alliances this way: "I use the term alliance to mean cooperation between groups that produces better results than can be gained from a transaction."[1]

Consulting group Booz-Allen uses a more lengthy definition:

> We define a strategic alliance as a cooperative arrangement between two or more companies where: A common strategy is developed in unison and a win–win attitude is adopted by all parties. The relationship is reciprocal, with each partner prepared to share specific strengths with each other, thus lending power to the enterprise. A pooling of resources, investment and risks occurs for mutual (rather than individual) gain.[2]

Since there is often confusion between the terms partnership and alliance, a means of distinguishing the two is useful. There are many distinguishing characteristics but these are the most commonly recognized ones.[3] In strategic alliances, there is greater uncertainty and ambiguity. The manner in which value is created – and how partners capture it – is not predetermined. The partner relationship may evolve in unpredictable ways. Today's ally may be tomorrow's rival – or a current rival in another market arena. Managing the relationship over time is more important than the initial design. Initial agreements have less to do with success than with adaptability to change.

LEGAL PARTNERSHIPS

Another kind of partnership is the legal entity called a partnership. There will be a brief section devoted to this too, but smart readers know that *legal advice should come from lawyers* – so I will only give you the practical highlights of a partnership as a legal entity.

CRM/PRM (Customer Relationship Management/Partner Relationship Management)

CRM is a popular acronym ("buzzword") for age-old processes translated to the new computer/Web-based economy. Its devotees describe CRM as "the overall process of marketing, sales, and service within any organization." Others describe it differently: "a business strategy to get, grow, and retain the right customers, leading to long-term profitability."

PRM is a subset of CRM, and is "the application of relationship management strategies and technologies to the unique needs of indirect sales channels." CRM and PRM systems are supposed to help businesses develop and sustain profitable customer/channel partner relationships – and maybe they do.

> "Customer Relationship Management (CRM) is a business strategy to select and manage customer relationships to optimize long-term value to an enterprise. CRM requires a customer-centric business philosophy and culture to support effective marketing, sales and service processes across all direct and indirect customer interaction channels. CRM software applications can enable effective Customer Relationship Management, provided an enterprise has the right strategy, leadership, and culture."
>
> *www.CRMGuru.com*

Companies are investing in CRM in hopes of becoming more effective in their selling while gaining competitive differentiation in a world where pricing is globally transparent and products become commodities overnight. *But there is no replacement for good old-fashioned customer relationships – between people!*

Key functional areas of CRM include:

» Marketing automation – Targets the best customers, manages marketing campaigns, generates quality leads, and shares the information easily.
» Sales automation – Supports the selling process from lead qualification to closing the business.
» Customer service – Resolves customer issues responsively after the sale, building customer satisfaction and loyalty.
» E-commerce – Handles the transaction online, as a seamless extension of the sales process.

> "Outsourcing non-core services forces companies to rethink their basic competencies and develop relationships with suppliers to provide the others."
>
> *Robert Rosen*[4]

OUTSOURCING

Outsourcing is a strategic decision to obtain goods or services from independent organizations outside of a company's legal boundaries; to purchase goods or services instead of making or doing them.

Outsourcing is still most prevalent in administrative and support activities, and not as often used in the "value-creating" ones. However, in recent years, more companies have formed strategic outsourcing partnerships in what were primary value creation areas. This comes about as companies decide to concentrate on what they do best and outsource the rest.

STRATEGIC OUTSOURCING

New partnerships now result in value-creating activities being outsourced to third-party logistics provider partners like UPS, or FedEx, or contract manufacturer partners like Jabil, Flextronics, Solectron, and many others. These partners' excellence in their respective specialties have reshaped the old sourcing model.

The newest business concept uses strategic partnerships with certain suppliers to provide the highest level of integrated value – based on close-knit partner linkage and rapid response capabilities. In some cases, well-known companies like Sara Lee have outsourced all manufacturing in favor of becoming a marketer and distributor/systems integrator. This is a role Nike has played almost since its inception. While some of these may turn out to be alliances, joint ventures, or simply arm's-length transactions, one simply doesn't know at the outset.

PARTNERSHIP AGREEMENT

This is a written agreement outlining the expectations, goals, and objectives of the partners as they initiate a partnership. It is often the basis for a legal partnership, and a communications tool to help organizations understand the nature and scope of a partnership, including allocation of risks, resources, and rewards as well as the assignment of responsibilities.

NOTES

1 Lewis, Jordan (1990) *Partnerships for Profit: Structuring and Managing Strategic Alliances*. The Free Press, New York.

2 Booz-Allen & Hamilton (1993) "A Practical Guide to Alliances: Leapfrogging the Learning Curve." New York.
3 Adapted from Doz, Yves & Hamel, Gary (1998) *Alliance Advantage*. Harvard Business School Press, Boston, MA.
4 Rosen, Robert (2000) *Global Literacies*. Simon & Schuster, New York.

Evolution

This chapter explains the origins of partnering in terms of human, organizational, political, and corporate settings. It also describes new forms of partnerships and challenges of the twenty-first century.

DEFINITIONS – A BEGINNING

To begin to understand the evolution of partnerships, a definition is the best starting point. Since the primary participants in the partnership are the partners, let's start there.

> Definition of **partner** (noun) One that is united or associated with another or others in an activity or a sphere of common interest, especially: **a**. A member of a business partnership. **b**. A spouse. **c**. Either of two persons dancing together. **d**. Sports & Games. One of a pair or team in a sport or game, such as tennis or bridge. verb, intransitive: To work or perform as a partner.[1]
> [Middle English partener, alteration (influenced by part, part), of parcener, parcener. See parcener.]
> Definition of **part·ner·ship** (pärt'ner-shîp) (noun) A relationship between individuals or groups that is characterized by mutual cooperation and responsibility, as for the achievement of a specified goal. The state of being a partner.[2]

FROM THE BEGINNING OF HUMANS

Where did partnerships begin? Probably with the beginning of humans as intelligent beings. The earliest records seem to show that humans found the need for help – for partners – almost from the very beginning. Even the Bible confirms that God, in His wisdom of creation, realized that Adam needed a partner, and thus created Eve. Whether in monogamous or polygamous societies, men and women formed the earliest of partnerships.

Lone hunters quickly learned that their life spans were shortened noticeably by the lack of a partner to watch their backs. Soon small bands of hunters roamed the virgin forests and plains for game – groups of the earliest partners. Meanwhile, back in the earliest settlements, the women who stayed home began to collaborate on doing some of the work. Some were better at making soap. Others spun the yarn and wove the fabric. While all might learn the rudiments of each craft, skills-based partnerships soon evolved and trading of skills and the output began.

Nearly all of folklore and literature describes partners working together to achieve more than either could alone. Rather than go through a historical litany of partners through the ages, I will jump to more modern times and the development of companies based on partnering. Described below is a time line of some notable partnerships through the ages.

Pre-1800 ... the agrarian era

Many agreements existed in the era from the 1500s to the 1700s, but most of these were not true partnerships. This was an era when power ruled and absolute power ruled absolutely. Whether it was the feudal system with its serf labor in Europe or slavery in the early days of America, the idea of partnerships was applied in limited cases and was largely the province of the wealthy. The partnerships that existed depended on the integrity of a few men who entered into them. It was not uncommon for pioneers to partner among themselves, and their handshake was usually their bond.

What was uncommon was for men of power to partner – at least in any meaningful sense – with anyone. Power had emerged through the ages as the dominant force. Economic power, military power, the power of force, and the power granted by wealth dictated who did what and for whom. Partnerships were rare, as were true democracies. The United States with its Constitution was one of the first federalist democracies, and as it grew in size, wealth, and influence, the concepts of democratic partnerships grew with it. Like most US concepts, many of the predecessor ideas originated in Europe. Others grew from necessity and the tribal nature of humans.

1800 ... the pre-industrial era

Earliest trappers turned over their goods to partners – traders – who played a valuable role in bringing the skins to market. Gold miners, who searched so hard for the precious metal, had then to find partners – assayers, smelters, and so forth – to buy and convert their ore to a useful form. As farms grew and individual farmers could no longer tend all of the fields, they too had to turn to partners. One could argue about the fairness of using "share croppers" (in the Unites States) or its predecessor, the feudal/serf system in Europe, but each was a primitive form of partnership in its era – albeit an unbalanced one.

Modern contract farmers think nothing about using (migrant) labor to pick crops and bring them to market on a seasonal basis. There are those who would condemn such "uses" of poorly paid partners, but in the free market relationship each partner gives something and gets something in return. And, since the abolition of slavery in most of the world, they do so freely, even if the roles are unequal.

The Native Americans, "the Indians," were among the most likely partners, as they attempted to survive in their own unique way, forging agreements over the ceremony of smoking the "peace pipe." Although many tribes warred on each other, many others partnered for their mutual benefit.

The Indians made the mistake of trusting the "white man" and as settlers from the eastern United States moved westward, it was the Indians who were the victims of broken partnership agreements – treaties made with the "white man." The era was one of ambivalence about whether military power or peaceful partnering made more sense. Since power was easier to use (if one had it), that method often won out.

Somewhat the same things were played out as governments worked together. Politics often spawned so-called partnerships or alliances, but many of these were not true partnerships. This definition from US author Ambrose Bierce (1842-1914) illustrates his thinly veiled contempt for political alliances:

> "Alliance. In international politics, the union of two thieves who have their hands so deeply inserted in each other's pockets that they cannot separately plunder a third."
> *Ambrose Bierce, The Devil's Dictionary (1881-1906)*[3]

Not everyone shared Bierce's cynicism about alliances and partnerships, as shown by the following serious quote from US statesman John Hay (1838-1905). Hay could see that to accomplish anything really meaningful, people would have to learn to partner.

> "All who think cannot but see there is a sanction like that of religion which binds us in partnership in the serious work of the world."
> *John Hay, Address, April 21, 1898, as ambassador in London, on Anglo-American relations*[4]

1900 ... the Industrial Revolution

Certainly the earliest forms of businesses quickly moved from sole proprietorships into partnerships. The Industrial Revolution created the need for businesses that were too complex to be the province of any one person or company. Even Henry Ford's vaunted company and its River Rouge (Detroit, MI) plant – in its time, the most vertically integrated company of its kind – finally had to depend on supplier partners.

The partnership was so much a part of the growth of business that some of the early competing US industrialists – Andrew Carnegie and J.P. Morgan – felt compelled to delineate their differences about partnerships.

> "Mr Morgan buys his partners; I grow my own."
> *Andrew Carnegie (1835-1919), US industrialist, philanthropist*[5]

The names of many of today's legendary companies reveal their heritage as partnerships. Daimler and Benz, the two inventors of the very first automobiles, joined forces to create a world-recognized auto company. Procter & Gamble, the leader in consumer packaged goods, and Sears, Roebuck & Company were two better known examples of partnerships that originated just prior to the turn of the twentieth century.

1930 ... the growth of corporations

Leading accounting firms were noted for and legally organized as partnerships. Mergers have blurred the original names into alphabet soup, but certainly most people recall Ernst & Whinney, which became Ernst & Young, and Peat, Marwick & Mitchell, later KPMG, or Price-Waterhouse, or Coopers & Lybrand. In the interest of not being out of date before out of print, I won't even try to link together the new names. The point is that all of these were, and in most cases still are, "partnerships" both technically (legally) and actually.

Large law firms are well known for their multi-named partnerships. So also are investment banks and advertising agencies. Many of these became partners in recent decades because of mergers and acquisitions, but the important point is that they were, indeed, founded as partnerships from their very inception. The topic of partnerships failing was addressed by leading authors as well. This wisdom applies equally well today as it did almost four decades ago.

> "By the time a partnership dissolves, it has dissolved."
> *John Updike (b. 1932), US author, critic. Couples, ch. 5 (1968)*[6]

Strategic partnering was active in corporate circles in this era as well. In 1943, Dow Chemical and Corning Glass partnered, forming an independent company to market a jointly developed, innovative product based on a substance called silicone. Such partnerships were becoming increasingly popular.

1950 and post-World War II – UN, NATO, and ... hamburgers

As business partnerships were evolving in the post-World War II era, so also were alliances between groups of countries with common interests. The United Nations was formed in 1945 to promote peace, security, and economic development. Proposals to establish an organization of nations for maintenance of world peace led to the United Nations Conference on International Organization at San Francisco, April 25 to June 26, 1945, where the Charter of the United Nations was drawn up. It was signed on June 26 by 50 nations, and by Poland, one of the original 51 UN members, on October 15, 1945. The charter came into effect on October 24, 1945, upon ratification by the permanent members of the Security Council and a majority of other signatories.

The UN's purpose was stated as

> "to maintain international peace and security; to develop friendly relations among nations; to achieve international cooperation in solving economic, social, cultural, and humanitarian problems and in promoting respect for human rights and fundamental freedoms; to be a center for harmonizing the actions of nations in attaining these common ends."[7]

While this is not exactly a partnership *per se*, it was as close as large political assemblages could come at this time.

The North Atlantic Treaty Organization (NATO) was created by treaty in 1949. Members as of 1995 were Belgium, Canada, Denmark, France, Germany, Greece, Iceland, Italy, Luxembourg, the Netherlands, Norway, Portugal, Spain, Turkey, the United Kingdom, and the United States. The members agreed to settle disputes by peaceful means; to develop their individual and collective capacity to resist armed attack; to regard an attack on one as an attack on all; and to take necessary action to repel an attack under Article 51 of the UN Charter.

The NATO structure consisted of a Council and a Military Committee of three commands (Allied Command Europe, Allied Command Atlantic, Allied Command Channel) and the Canada–US Regional Planning Group. With the dissolution of the Soviet Union and the end of the Cold War in the early 1990s, NATO members sought to modify the organization's mission, putting greater stress on political action and creating a rapid deployment force to react to local crises.[8]

The growth and success of McDonald's, the world's largest and best-known fast-food restaurant chain, would have been impossible without partnerships. McDonald's simply couldn't obtain enough high-quality, uniform meat, buns, packaging, etc., by purchasing from hundreds of sources scattered around the United States, and then later around the globe. What it did instead was to form semi-captive partnerships with companies that would provide consistent quality for the volume of food and supplies necessary to grow globally.

Companies like Martin-Brower and Schwarz Paper are inextricably tied to McDonald's and have grown based on those partnership ties. Has it always been easy? Of course not! Like all large purchasers, McDonald's at times became overly demanding or unreasonable, but through the decades, these partnerships hung together because it was better to struggle together than to struggle separately. Coca-Cola has also been a long-term (but non-captive) McDonald's partner, supplying beverages to the chain's stores around the world.

1980 ... the modern giant corporations

Some suppliers to giants like Sears, Wal-Mart, or Home Depot may feel that they are as subservient to those masters as the migrant workers were to the farmers of an earlier era. The 1970s were an era of giant corporations emerging and forming partnerships with suppliers. In these so-called partnerships, suppliers were often second-class partners dominated by the larger and stronger customer partner. But life went on and partnerships continued to evolve – some still remain this way, but many do not.

A more recent partnership example is that of Chrysler Corporation (now DaimlerChrysler) and the partnerships it formed with suppliers in the 1990s. A *Harvard Business Review* article of the time called it an "American Keiretsu." The Japanese have long used the "keiretsu" – their own form of dependent partnership – to tie suppliers to large manufacturers. This tight relationship has provided Japan with an advantage in quality, proximity of suppliers, and coordination for the past several decades, and is one of the key ingredients in the vaunted "Lean Production" processes based on the Toyota Production System. This also worked very well for Chrysler in the 1990s.

> "Here is a key to alliances: Organizations that collaborate well on the inside have the skills needed for doing so on the outside. The opposite is equally true."
>
> *Jordan Lewis*

Unlike General Motors and Ford Motor Company, Chrysler's evolution left it with a much smaller, captive, in-house component supply network. While this was a disadvantage to Chrysler in the earlier decades, it became an advantage in the 1990s. As the captive supplier companies of GM and Ford became saddled with restrictive United Auto Workers (UAW) union work rules and exorbitant pay rates, Chrysler could turn to many independent suppliers for its parts needs. Many of these same suppliers had grown tired of bidding for GM or Ford work, only to find their best ideas stolen and the contracts awarded to captive (in-house) parts divisions.

Chrysler, in its hour of need, turned to the suppliers in much truer partnership approach. Led by Thomas Stallkamp, in its SCORE program, Chrysler urged suppliers to share new ideas and cost savings in return for increased volume. While Ignacio Lopez was beating up GM suppliers for cost savings (this was before he defected to VW), Chrysler was partnering in more of a two-way, win–win manner. The benefits were staggering. Chrysler's SCORE program led to billions of dollars of savings, but perhaps more importantly, provided innovative ideas and reduced lead times. Suddenly, Chrysler was beating its US competitors to market with better, more innovative products. Its scale/cost disadvantage was being offset by its supplier partnership benefits.

> "When it is possible to fully trust a partner, there is no need to control its behavior. Control comes into play only when trust is not present."[9]

While this history was unfolding in the auto industry, it was being paralleled in the retail trade in the United States. Sears developed a tightly controlled network of near captive and captive suppliers to support its growth in the 1960-1980 era. Later, in the 1980-1990 time frame, Wal-Mart emerged with a more collaborative partnership approach. While both could be very tough to deal with, and at times wielded power instead of partnering, Wal-Mart was by far the more collaborative organization. That collaborative behavior came from the leadership – first of Sam Walton, then David Glass, and now of Lee Scott and Tom Coughlin.

> "I personally see more consolidation: more partnerships, more strategic alliances, and more acquisitions."
> *Jac Nasser, Ford CEO, FORTUNE, December 18, 2000*

2000 ... the Internet era

One of the most explosive eras for partnerships and alliances has been the current one, since the widespread development of the World Wide Web and Web browsers in 1995. Literally hundreds of partnerships and alliances have been announced, formed, modified, disbanded, violated, and left in rubble as many erstwhile partners ceased to exist. Some few of them remain, and others have actually entered formal mergers. One of the most famous surviving partnership/mergers is AOL-Time Warner, including Netscape.

In periods of rapid technological development, the need for partners is increased. New technological developments make it difficult or impossible for companies to keep up, and thus they form partnerships or alliances in order to share knowledge, technology, networks, and skills.

If one were to attempt to map all of the interconnecting partnerships formed in the period from 1995 to 2000 as the Internet, e-commerce, and the dot-com revolution were developing, the chart would have changed daily and been so complex and intermingled as to be impossible to decipher.

Why is this the case? Because rapid change spawns new and different needs, making the choice of partners, the formation of partnerships, and their sustenance an incredibly dynamic situation. Such a situation must be constantly changing because the environment that it attempts to serve is constantly changing. I will expand on this further in a future chapter when I describe the value network.

> "The ability to attract partners and manage alliances, or as we prefer to call it, to be magnetic, is the new core competency of the networked age."
>
> Matthew Schifrin, FORBES.COM, The Best of The Web,
> May 21, 2001

GOVERNMENTS AND GLOBALIZATION = PARTNERS AND ALLIES MORE THAN EVER

In the case of national security, major countries like the United States have always needed allies. That is why there were many alliances formed around the time of World War II. As economies globalize, economic allies are needed too, and the boundary between military power and economic power continues to blur.

In the absence of the Cold War between the superpowers, there is a need for allies to band together in order that rogue states can be controlled for the common good. No single country wants to spend its money or resources to be the world's policeman – and that includes the United States – in spite of its tendencies to the contrary.

This means that one of the largest challenges faced by our world is who to partner, how to form those alliances, and what to do when the inevitable friction between partners arises. Actually, making partnerships work is not just a business problem. It is a global, political, socio-economic, human problem of epic proportions. It seems that over time, the more things change, the more they remain the same.

In *The Lexus and the Olive Tree*, Thomas Friedman describes it from his perspective:

> "That is why in the system of globalization the biggest challenge for American leadership is to sort out which problems it can still shape alone, through classical state-to-state military deterrence, and which problems it can shape today only with partners."

Clearly, partnering is a "world-class" challenge on a global scale.

Totally different kinds of partnership challenges

Now partnerships have begun to take on whole new meanings, such as the one shown in the paragraph below. As society changes, governments and companies must be alert to the changes and how those changes affect them. Partnerships are formed to do all sorts of things as social changes occur!

> **PARTNERS TASK FORCE**
>
> **Audience: gay and lesbian couples**
> Dedicated to the idea that "all families are created equal," this page [http://www.eskimo.com/~demian/partners.html] is a project of the Partners Task Force (PTF) for Gay and Lesbian Couples, located in Seattle, Washington. According to PTF, "counter to many myths, more than 50% of the gay and lesbian community is in a relationship." Acknowledging that stereotypes can harm the gay and lesbian community, this page promotes a different, more stable image of the reality of gay and lesbian couples and families. You can see articles on same-sex marriage, legal and medical issues (including how to get a Medical Emergency Card), and more.[10]

The preceding example may not be the most popular one. But many new kinds of partnerships are being formed in just the time it has taken to read this section – and not all of them in businesses – but all of them eventually affect business. To make partnerships work in business, it is imperative that managers and executives consider all of the dynamic issues that might be involved. Human interaction is at the root of partnerships and the issue of gay rights is becoming a major bone of contention in employee rights issues, and thus a factor in employee partnerships.

Employers are also faced with many other special interest groups/partnerships that take action based on deep-seated feelings such as abortion rights/reimbursement for costs, immigration policies/quotas, health care issues, gay marriages/benefit issues, and many, many more. Understanding the impact of these issues on "partnerships" of all kinds is a critical factor in making employee partnerships work in the twenty-first century.

An example to emulate – Southwest Airlines

One of the most positive examples of partner relationships in the past decade is the one between Southwest Airlines and its employees. The company's success has been attributed to many factors – operational efficiency, customer friendliness, consistency – but all of these are the result of one other factor. Southwest Airlines has invested in the relationship with its employees and it is these employees that make all of the other things happen. By making its employees true, trusting partners, the company has made it possible for its employees to make its customers partners too. When this happens, other good things start to happen. The power of partnerships is immense, but there is no "faking it" – it must be done right.

Colleen Barrett, Southwest Airlines' newly appointed chief operating officer (COO), frames the challenge simply but brilliantly when she says:

> "We are very proud of our employee relationships. We treat people with respect. But we would take a strike if it goes down to it – especially if it was about money and we simply couldn't concede without hurting all employees by the decision. We are loving but very realistic and very pragmatic."

What a sincerely honest position this is – and the right one.

There are few things about business and life that are certain – perhaps death and taxes are two of them. A third certainty is the continued need for partnerships between people, businesses, and among groups of people in all walks of life. That means "making partnerships work" will certainly be an important thing to know for the future, no matter what your field of work, or how complex the issues are that must be faced.

Just as partnerships have evolved over time, so also must the sophistication with which executives recognize and deal with the issues inhibiting success in forming and sustaining partnerships.

"Mature companies can reinvent themselves, small outfits can leapfrog competitors, and firms of all sizes can partner to enter new markets."

Matthew Schifrin

NOTES

1 *The American Heritage® Dictionary of the English Language, Third Edition* copyright © 1992 by Houghton Mifflin Company. Electronic version licensed from INSO Corporation. All rights reserved.
2 Ibid.
3 *The Columbia Dictionary of Quotations* is licensed from Columbia University Press. Copyright © 1993, 1995 by Columbia University Press. All rights reserved.
4 Ibid.
5 Quoted in: Burton J. Hendrick (1932) *Life of Andrew Carnegie*, vol. 1, ch. 15, sect. 2. *The Columbia Dictionary of Quotations* is licensed from Columbia University Press. Copyright © 1993, 1995 by Columbia University Press. All rights reserved.
6 Ibid.
7 *The World Almanac® and Book of Facts 1996* is licensed from Funk & Wagnalls Corporation. Copyright © 1995 by Funk & Wagnalls Corporation. All rights reserved.
8 Ibid.
9 Das, T.K. & Teng, Bing-Sheng (1998) "Between trust and control: developing confidence in partner cooperation in alliances." *Academy of Management Review*, Baruch College, CUNY.
10 Microsoft Bookshelf Internet Directory 96-7, ed. Kevin Savetz.

The E-Dimension

This chapter looks at the impact of technological change, the formation, and dissolution of many e-partnerships. It describes a few partnership initiatives that survived the shakeout stage of the e-dimension.

THE BROWSER AND WEB

The Internet exploded on the business scene in 1994 with the development of the first commercially viable Web browser, Mosaic, at the University of Illinois in the United States. Mosaic's team of inventors, led by Marc Andreeson, found entrepreneur Jim Clark shortly after he sold his stake in Silicon Graphics. The Palo Alto meeting between these two led to a partnership that touched off one of the greatest "booms" of the twentieth century, even if it did not start until the waning years of the century. The product of this partnership was the Netscape Navigator Web browser.

The Internet had been in existence for a couple of decades, but its use had been limited mostly to government and universities using arcane and technically complex means of finding each other and searching for information. The World Wide Web evolved when the browser and the cataloging of sites by search engines made practical use of the Internet not only possible but also desirable.

What ensued was a "rush" like the "gold rush" era of centuries earlier – but this time it was to get into the new technology and capitalize on it. New companies sprung up like weeds after a spring rain. Since the technology and its application were all new, no one was good enough at all aspects of it. This led to a veritable avalanche of partnerships, alliances, joint ventures, and subsequent collapses.

"Over the course of a few years, a new communications technology annihilated distance and shrank the world faster and further than ever before. A world-wide communications network whose cables spanned continents and oceans, it revolutionized business practices and gave rise to new forms of crime."
   Steve Woolgar – talking about the telegraph in 1840, not the Internet

AN EXPLOSION OF PARTNERSHIPS AND ALLIANCES

Partnerships were easy to form. Speed was of the essence, and the buzz of a hot partnership deal being announced lifted already inflated stock prices higher and higher. Everybody was "partnering" with everybody else on something. Alliances were everywhere. The news broke daily, and grew until even the most devoted researcher could not keep up with it. Trying to chart the interlocked partnerships and relationships created a "spaghetti bowl" of interconnections. The typical Silicon Valley conversation might have gone like this: "I'll trade you some of my inflated stock for your inflated stock, we'll both book nice revenues from it, and the partnership is formed. Let's issue a press release."

Unfortunately, what goes up must come down – and the faster it goes up, the faster it crashes when the fuel runs out. This time the fuel was cash. Most of these Internet startups had little or no plans to make a profit. Just get going fast and ride the wave. Do an initial public offering (IPO) and be worth millions. Partner with the big "old economy" companies like AT&T and IBM and there is instant credibility.

> "In the end, this will probably be like the telephone ... this huge new revolution that didn't make much difference to existing social structures."
>
> *Steve Woolgar*

THE CRASHES OF MANY

The problem was, once the initial cash ran out, so did the rocket fuel. The smart old-line companies were more careful about who they got into bed with, and this meant many of the new alliances were incestuous – putting together two or more new entities all of which were burning through cash at an amazing rate. Partnerships between two or three companies that are destined to fail are like no partnerships at all. The Internet, dot-com, and e-commerce frenzy became so great that it spawned a valuation "bubble" in the world's stock markets that was bound to burst. And burst it did.

The landscape was littered with ruined companies and vacated partnerships. Debts and promises blew away like bubbles in the wind. Some partnerships still remain. America Online, one of the portal pioneers, made it through the turmoil and used its valuable stock to merge with media giant Time Warner. Amazon.com, the premier retail site, has grown from books to many categories of goods by using partnerships to access secondary distribution, but it has yet to turn any kind of profit without accounting gymnastics.

TOYS "R" US AND AMAZON.COM – A PARTNERSHIP THAT MAKES SENSE

Amazon.com's partnership with toy retailer Toys "R" Us (TRU) is the prototype for the partnership of an old economy and new economy company. Amazon.com broke a new frontier in B2C (Business to Consumer) with its pioneering work as a bookseller. The problem is that amazon.com keeps spending ahead of its sales and has yet to come close to making a profit. There are those (the author included) who question whether amazon.com's original model could work at all in the long term.

However, a partnership between an experienced and established "bricks & mortar" company and amazon.com is a good one. TRU attempted to launch its own Web initiative twice – once on its own and once in a partnership with Benchmark Partners. Each failed because it (and its management and board) could not come to grips with the issue of cannibalizing its own retail store sales.

The problem with the toy business is that it is seasonal and volatile. Missed sales at Christmas due to stock-outs end up being lost sales. Guess wrong on the inventory, and there is big trouble.

Meanwhile, in the early dot-com explosion, e-Toys and toysmart.com were getting all the publicity, the media hype, and a concerning amount of online sales. Yet neither of these two had the economic staying power nor the long-term business plan that a TRU – amazon partnership did.

So, while TRU struggled with its Web presence, amazon.com struggled with its fulfillment costs and inventory management; e-Toys and toysmart.com struggled just to exist. When amazon.com and TRU joined forces in a partnership, a strong new model was born. Amazon.com provides the front end – taking orders and handling the transaction from the Web information technology side; TRU, with its network of retail stores and large sales base, providing the inventory cushion and fulfillment – through already existing distribution centers.

Disney quickly grabbed toysmart.com but the combination was not the right chemistry. Disney's tradition-bound, large-company mentality was diametrically opposed to toysmart.com's fast and loose approach to the business. When Disney attempted to conserve toysmart.com's dwindling cash by insisting that it concentrate its advertising on Disney's ABC television, toysmart.com resisted. Finally, while the two tugged back and forth, the cash ran out.

As amazon.com and TRU joined forces, the toy business that naturally flowed through this powerful combination of the premier global toy retailer and the premier Web retailer drained valuable volume from remaining dot-com toy retailer e-Toys.

However, e-Toys had a bit more staying power than toysmart.com, though it just ran out of cash in the 2001 post-Christmas sales doldrums. A vast percentage of toy business is done in the fourth quarter of the year. Without any additional revenue to sustain it through the slower parts of the year, e-toys was finished, and its inventory and customer list divided like spoils among new and old economy merchants.

The best partnerships are win-win, and use the relative strengths of each partner to make up for the other partner's weaknesses. That is exactly what happened here. It is a model that amazon.com will use again and again - if it is smart - and build still more win-win partnerships.

Evidence of the viability of this model is that amazon.com''s bookseller/competitor Borders turned over its Web-based operation to amazon.com - just like TRU did. In this case, however, amazon.com is already in the book fulfillment business, so it will manage more of the supply chain than in the TRU partnership. One thing is clear - the path to success in the e-dimension is paved with partnerships.

A NEW E-BUSINESS MODEL

High tech, high touch, high speed, high risk, high profit - these are all partnership and business and strategic issues. So your partner is 'wired' to you. Great! Or is it? No more hiding the late production and short inventory on a critical item. No more fuzzy answers about when that order will ship or when that service will be completed. Are you ready for that – partner?

> "By 2005, nearly half of all Web-based commerce will be collaborative in nature."
>
> *The Gartner Group*

The era of the Internet has moved the connectivity and openness of information sharing to a whole new level. In days gone by, people could "bend the truth" without getting caught. Not any more! Now the elements of trust and trustworthiness are being put to the ultimate test. The question now will not be "when is the shipment I need going to arrive?" The question will be "what are you going to do to get me what I need in time, because the way your schedules are set up now, that is not going to happen?" Kind of a different tone – right?

But, if the parts of the system that are supposed to be working ahead of this time are doing their job, perhaps that question will be asked much less frequently. Internet technologies and close-knit partnerships now make it possible for partners to truly collaborate on planning, forecasting, and making adjustments throughout the supply chain, not just in one factory or delivery process. If the retail trade's effort on CPFR – that stands for Collaborative Planning, Forecasting, and Requirements – works broadly like it is beginning to in a few places, then a whole new era of partnerships and value network management is at hand.

NETWORKED INCUBATORS AND THE NEW ECONOMY

A new partnership-building business model

> "When properly designed, networked incubators combine the best of two worlds – the scale and scope of large, established corporations and the entrepreneurial spirit of small venture-capital firms – all while providing unique networking

benefits. Because of this combination, we believe that networked incubators represent a fundamentally new organization model that is especially well suited for creating value and wealth in the new economy.

"The distinguishing feature of a networked incubator is that it has mechanisms to foster partnership among start-up teams and other successful Internet-oriented firms, thus facilitating the flow of knowledge and talent across companies and forging of marketing and technology relationships between them. With the help of such an incubator, start-ups can network to obtain resources, and partner with others quickly, allowing them to establish themselves in the marketplace ahead of competitors."

Morten Hansen, Henry Chesbrough, Nitin Nohria, and Donald Sull (2000) "Networked incubators - hothouses of the new economy." Harvard Business Review, September-October

INFORMATION FOR ALL – PROCTER & GAMBLE'S "PROJECT M"

Household products giant Procter & Gamble is taking advantage of the e-dimension in a new venture intended to share employee know-how. By forming a new company named Magnifi and then joining forces with it, Procter & Gamble hopes to put its collective knowledge at the fingertips of its brand managers. Magnifi will develop computer programs to manage and speed how employees share information in a project called Project Enterprise Marketing Management ("Project m").

Brand managers at Procter & Gamble, like their counterparts in all kinds of companies, spend a lot of time on unproductive busy-work like confirming that an advertising agency has received the latest revisions to a new commercial or following up on small details of a project. There is usually a great deal of knowledge that resides somewhere in the collective minds of the company employees, but where, and what is it?

"Project m" will store a library of Procter & Gamble know-how making it possible for a new brand manager to easily and quickly find out how predecessors handled campaigns for launching a new brand. The managers can discover how a brand is being marketed in other countries, thus increasing global synergies. Lacking the software and the technology, it would be difficult or impossible for these managers to access this kind of information on a comprehensive basis. One brand manager estimates that she spends 60% of her time on just coordinating details of a project, and that "Project m" can cut that time in half.

Ultimately Procter & Gamble will face two challenges for this powerful new initiative to reach its full potential. The first is that major system rollouts are difficult, and shown by problems many companies have in enterprise resource planning (ERP) installations. The second difficulty is that for the system to have the maximum potential results, it will be necessary for Procter & Gamble to have the participation of its supplier partners. As in most e-dimensions, partnerships that are collaborative efforts are necessary to maximize the benefit from the technologies employed.

> "Let's admit first that 'relationship' is one of the most abused words in business. Dot-com CEOs like to say 'We have relationships with two million customers,' but that's usually a lie. It means two million customers have placed at least one order."
> *Geoffrey Colvin (2001) "Shaking hands on the Web."*
> *FORTUNE, May 14*

PARTNERS ADD VISIBILITY AND PERSPECTIVE

Further evidence of this e-trend is the Gartner Group, a leader in e-business consulting and research, sponsoring a "summit" meeting under the heading "The Power of e-Partnerships." As their premise they state:

> "These days, business leadership means the ability to see what's coming next for your organization ... In the next twelve months ... initiatives involving Web-enabled interaction between enterprises, their customers, trading partners and employees will surpass e-commerce as a top business priority. **By 2005, nearly**

half of all Web-based commerce will be collaborative in nature."

This prediction in bold shows the importance of partnerships and the e-dimension working together to maximize the success of businesses all over the globe.

Information systems and service giant IBM confirms the importance of such initiatives in its statement, "IBM's starting a partnership program with solution providers in customer relationship management (CRM) and supply chain management procurement technology." When IBM decides it must partner with erstwhile competitors Siebel and Ariba, then clearly the area is growing in importance and in influence.

PARTNERING WITH COMPETITORS

The trend of partnering with would-be competitors is mirrored in the announcement of i2 Technologies partnership with iPlanet, a joint venture of Sun Microsystems and AOL-Time Warner. This is a partnership to the second power, which gives i2 the underlying technology to launch new products over the Web. The new technologies will permit tailoring Websites to better match customer preferences, and extend their accessibility.

Traditional CRM packages don't let companies share information from Websites with their suppliers. With this kind of extended relationship management system, it is possible to see further into the supply chain than previously. More visibility means a greater opportunity for improved coordination and a reduction in waste and lead time. The ultimate question is whether these multi-partner latch-ups will stay together and function effectively, or whether competitive friction will tear them apart.

EXCHANGES AND MARKETPLACE

Transora

The final e-dimension partnership issue is the one raised by so many of the highly publicized B2B (Business to Business) exchanges or marketplaces. Two of them that bear scrutiny are Transora and Covisint.

Transora was born of notes on a napkin during a meeting of executives from consumer goods companies Kraft, Kellogg, Campbell Soup, and Nabisco. Covisint, the giant auto parts marketplace formed by DaimlerChrysler, Ford, and GM had just been announced, and a common thought rippled through the gathering: "why can't we do that?"

What came of this question is a 250-person operation with the goal of creating a massive Web-based hub for manufacturers to trade information, logistics, and goods with suppliers and retailers around the world. Transora hoped to strike uniform industry-wide deals, cutting costs for both suppliers and buyers. The problem is that by mid-2001, Transora had gone through over half its startup funding and it was still struggling with the age-old problem – namely, fragmentation of ideas, methods, desires, and plans. People just can't seem to agree on specifics nearly as well as on vague generalities. This is the big challenge with partnering. As architect Mies Van De Rohe said, "God is in the details."

Transora will pick the "low hanging fruit" like combined buying for supplies, and a few basic auctions. But standardizing the whole industry is a much tougher proposition. There are literally thousands of products, and millions of variations. Even in the relatively mature process of EDI (Electronic Data Interchange), which has been in widespread use for a decade or more, human error is the weak link. Almost a third of all orders have some kind of error that requires human intervention. Standardizing this kind of inaccurate process will be a nightmare. Perhaps the best hope for Transora lies in promoting and enabling a much wider use of CPFR, since this process creates an inherently greater degree of cooperation, standardization and efficiency.

But even this won't be easy, because almost two-thirds of retailer's forecasting is still done via telephone interaction between people! According to Martha Uhlhorn, VP of e-commerce for Earthgrains, a St Louis (Missouri) based baked goods company, "The technology's easy, and the people are hard ... and the technology's not that easy." And if that is not enough of an obstacle, the other end of the supply chain looms as an even more daunting challenge. Retailers, the last link in the supply chain before consumers, are having their own doubts about Transora. Retailers have organized their own companies – WorldWide Retail Exchange, led by Target and Supervalu, and GlobalNetX-change created by Sears and Kroger. Then there is Wal-Mart which goes its own way and is big enough to do it all alone. Transora could be left out in the cold with little reason for existing if the retailers "freeze it out."

Covisint

It seems that for all of its press buzz, Covisint is having its own problems. First it went over a year with no CEO, then when one was hired, it was someone with no auto industry experience. This damaged the outlook for most supplier participants. Few of them wanted a techno-consultant for the CEO. Further, once the exchange has squeezed out the weak suppliers, and leveled the pricing field, what comes next? Will Ford, GM, and DaimlerChrysler really be satisfied buying the same things at the same deals? Not in your lifetime they won't. Each will be trying to gain some competitive advantage, as they should. Ultimately, the good suppliers will choose sides and cut deals outside the exchange, and this will weaken the entire foundation of the concept.

The future ... is still being formed

Beware the bewitching attractiveness of the marketplace exchanges. Some will work, but most will not. They make great news for the business press, but they are not proven as great for business. The savings from transaction streamlining will be realized, but the behavioral changes will come much more slowly. Why? Because there is more to it than technology – there is trust required for partnerships to work, and trust is slow coming in the e-dimension or any other dimension.

> "Global business moves at a much faster pace today. Strategic alliances help companies keep up. They are not merely an alternative, they are a necessity. The Web has awakened big companies to this new reality."
>
> *Matthew Schifrin*

The Global Dimension

Partnerships are discussed in this chapter in terms of the global value network. Managers need to be aware of how myriad events and situations around the world impact every aspect of their business. An example of an evolving value network is provided.

THE VALUE NETWORK

In a speaking engagement over three years ago, I used the term *value network* to describe this new global business concept for the twenty-first century. In the value network, partnerships play a pivotal role, perhaps the most essential role! This chapter frames an often clichéd term, partnerships, in the context of a total global value network that we all know exists, but that we fail to comprehend most of the time. But we need to comprehend it all of the time – and start thinking that way fast.

Author Gary Hamel also uses the term "value network" in his latest book, *Leading the Revolution*, and while he uses it in a more limited sense, many of the points he makes are in agreement with my (larger) global use of the term.

> "The fourth component of the business model is the value network that surrounds the firm and which complements and amplifies the firm's own resources. ... Elements of the value network include suppliers, partners, and coalitions."
>
> *Gary Hamel*[1]

A few years ago, writing in the *Wall Street Journal*, Peter Drucker referred to the "Network Society." In his book *The Lexus and the Olive Tree*, Thomas Friedman refers to the "Electronic Herd" and the "Golden Straitjacket." The names matter less than the fact that there is "something" out there and whatever it's called, it influences everything else we do. I think the name value network is better than the other names. It is, after all, a global network of partnerships which work together to create and deliver value!

> "The answer is to understand that in a world of networks, individuals, companies, communities, consumers, activist groups, and governments all have the power to be shapers – to shape human value chains."
>
> *Thomas Friedman*[2]

THE INTERNET CHANGES EVERYTHING

Much has been written about "how the Internet changes everything," and how new business concepts are needed because of these changes. The problem is, the Internet doesn't change everything, but its global speed and reach changes so much that everything else must change to adapt. Every company must adjust for the changes driven by the Internet, telecommunications, computing, and the information revolution and its remarkable rates of change. It is impossible to make these adjustments without close-knit partnerships with a large group of constituents, all interacting in a total global network context.

> "Strategic alliances are a logical and timely response to intense and rapid changes in economic activity, technology, and globalization."
>
> *Yves Doz and Gary Hamel*

Fortunately, most of the old economy truths remain true. It is these old truths and their relationship with the new truths that we must understand and build upon. *The value network is an interactive combination of information, machines and people*. The information (and knowledge) is embedded in the minds of the people and stored and/or transmitted by the machines. The people cannot succeed without the machines and the machines without the people are worth little. None of them can realize their full potential unless some kind of voluntary partnerships are created to make them into an integrated whole.

> "... just as the [Berlin] Wall has fallen down, the good guys and bad guys have gone away – to be replaced by the web which is a series of relationships, all increasingly connected with no one really in charge ... The world is setting its own pace, and it's being set by all the people, not one individual."
>
> *Thomas Friedman*[3]

THE OLD AND NEW ECONOMICS

In centuries past, wealth was determined by the possession of land, labor, or capital – and each was exclusive to its owner. In this new era, information has become a principal determinant of wealth, and its ownership is non-exclusive. In fact, the more it is shared, the richer and more valuable it becomes to whomever ultimately puts it to productive use. Partnerships simply accelerate the enrichment of information-based knowledge, while the value network and its associated machines (and technology in general) spread it around the globe in seconds.

> "Organizations are less brick and mortar and more communities of networks these days."
>
> *Robert Rosen*[4]

In the twenty-first century, as in the latter stages of the twentieth century, value has been the principal determinant of competitive advantage and business success. Whoever offered the best value won over the competition. But value is a constantly shifting thing. To understand it is difficult. To learn, adapt, and evolve in order to provide the best value continuously are even more complex and difficult. I devoted an entire book, *The Shape Shifters – Continuous Change for Competitive Advantage* (Wiley, 1997) to this concept of constantly shifting value and how to capitalize on it.

It was that book and its ideas that made me vitally aware of the existence and power of the value network. The key elements of the value network are many and varied – but at least these (six) are the most critical, and they fall into three broad "classes." The classes are: the *concepts*, which combine management, knowledge, and leadership; the *components*, which tie together partners of all kinds with the information needed to create and deliver value; the *context*, which is the environmental, societal, and physical situation in which we all live, work, and operate businesses. Many of the other, subordinate parts that make up the value network are listed and highlighted in the elements below.

The concepts

This consists of (1) the *purpose* and *strategy* of the business and the associated elements of its (2) *operational execution*. Within this strategy and execution is the question of who to partner, and why, and then how to do it. The concepts also include the choices of the *structure*, the *processes*, the *culture*, and the *relationships* within and upon which value is created and delivered.

If this seems obvious, at one level it is. At another, there are secrets to success that are less obvious. Those few "secrets" that remain are based on four important "formulas" surrounding information and knowledge and the concept of synergy.

If I give you a dollar and you give me a dollar, we both still have a dollar. If I give you an idea, and you give me an idea, we each have *two* ideas. Unlike the old determinants of wealth which were exclusive to their owners, and could be "used up," this synergy of information – that it grows in value as it is shared and used – is the basis for these four formulas. These are non-mathematical formulas, but they are as true as the most logical of the quantitative sciences. The critical terms in these formulas are data, information, insight, knowledge, wisdom, and imagination applied to any product (or business model). Here is how the four synergistic formulas work in the concept of the value network.

» **Data + organization = information**. Most of us are swimming in data, but without a means to organize this data, it provides precious little information. The sheer amount of data often obscures the important information that will allow us to work on the right issues.
» **Information + insight = knowledge**. Even after a lot of information is available, only the addition of human insight transforms it into useful knowledge. Insight provides the context and perspectives necessary to understand what customers value and the relationships that are so important.
» **Knowledge + experience = wisdom**. Only by combining what was learned from the successes and failures of the past with the knowledge of the present can we hope to have any true perspective about the future. Downsizing has driven much of the experience based on history out of companies and this creates a great risk of repeating past mistakes.
» **Wisdom + imagination = genius**. Rarely do companies move to entirely new plateaus of excellence, because they are too invested in preserving and protecting the present successes. When they do make these breakthroughs, they are often handsomely profitable.

This requires a special touch, namely imagination – that almost indescribable blending of logic and emotion, of science and art, with child-like curiosity and adult determination to weave an entirely new fabric of a business or an industry.

The greatest successes in the application of the value network are those built on the elements of the concept and enriched by the synergistic power of these four formulas.

The components

These are made up of (3) the *markets* in which the business operates or which it serves however defined. Choosing the right *suppliers* and *customers* as partners in those markets and then forging the partnerships necessary to serve those customers better than competitors is what Gary Hamel calls the value network; and it is a critical part – but just a part – of the whole.

The participants include the aforementioned suppliers and *their suppliers*, customers and *their customers*, plus all of the *employees*, independent *contractors*, members of *corporate governance*, etc. This is the heart of partnerships in the value network. Much of it is often called the "supply chain" or "value chain," but it is far more of a complex, non-linear network than it is a simple chain of any sort.

The information and communications infrastructure (4) forms the central nervous system interconnecting the preceding parts of the network. This is a big part of what Friedman calls the basis for the "Electronic Herd." Without this central nervous system carrying the information, businesses and partnerships between them will fail and die. The information and communications system is also a synergistic catalyst, which accelerates the reactions that create and deliver value. This was amply described in the preceding section with the four formulas.

The financial investment and physical resources (land, labor, and capital of olden days) (5) that are required to produce or deliver the goods or services by which revenues, net earnings, with positive ROIs or EVAs, are created. These are essential to sustain the entire value network. Understanding how "score is kept" in the value network is also critical.

Accounting systems that are so rigid in many developed countries are far from that in developing economies. Practices and disciplines vary widely around the globe, making seemingly comparable information misleading or useless. This dichotomy of quantitative information, which is qualitatively dangerous, is just one element of the value network that must be understood. Partners in these countries can provide the resources needed to understand this. No one and no company can survive and thrive without enough of the right kinds of resources. Special partners are often a rich source of these resources.

The value network – another perspective

"The elements of the Value Network include suppliers, partners and coalitions," says Gary Hamel.[5]

» Suppliers – typically reside up the value chain from the producer. Consider how effectively you use suppliers as a source of new ideas. Do you think they are integral to your business? Do you gain competitive advantage from the way you manage your supplier connection? Are your goals aligned with theirs?
» Partners – typically supply critical components to a final product. This is a more horizontal relationship than a vertical supplier. Do you look at the world as a reservoir of competencies which might complement yours? Do you use partners to "punch more than your own weight?" How can you better use partners to be more flexible, more focused, and create first to market speed?
» Coalitions – require a company to join forces with others for innovation, especially where the investment is high or the complexity great. Coalition members can become more than partners, sharing in the risk and reward of an industry revolution.

The context

Last, but certainly not least, is the external environment of the value network. It surrounds and influences all of the other parts in profound ways. Unless this part is considered in the entire value network consideration, the other parts will not work properly.

The *governmental*, *economic*, and *societal structures* (6) in which the businesses operate and compete are a major part of what Friedman describes as "DOSCapitol" – the "operating system" by which economies and countries control themselves and fuel their growth (or don't).

The environment in which organizations exist and the "operating system" they use determine which kinds of partners they need to survive and prosper. The economies and societies of the world with all of their governments, practices, laws, rituals, mores, and uniquely infinite variety are a part of the value network's "Context."

> "We define partner cooperation as the willingness of a partner firm to pursue mutually compatible interests in the alliance rather than act opportunistically."[6]

PARTNERSHIPS ARE KEY TO IT ALL

How does all this influence making partnerships work? It influences partnerships totally and throughout, because "the value network" is *the ultimate global partnership system*. Like a galaxy full of solar systems, separate, smaller value networks exist all over the world and are part of a giant, global value network. Their complexity is now evident by the richness of the concepts, the number and magnitude of the components, the variety of the context, and how partnerships are interwoven through and through them all.

Could this overwhelm you? Maybe so! Dare you let it? Emphatically no! Why? Because this is merely a "listing" of all of the interconnected elements among which businesses currently build and manage partnerships for survival and success. Think of it as a giant Yellow Pages of partnership opportunities and potential. "Let your fingers do the walking," not through the pages of paper, but on the keyboard of a computer, through the digits and bandwidth of the Internet, around the globe and back!

AN OPEN, TRANSPARENT WORLD[7]

This networked world is by definition an open, transparent world. Leaders must be community builders. By creating a climate of trust and teamwork, they focus three key strategies: managing knowledge, developing networks, and building alliances.

- » Managing knowledge – Globally literate leaders know that knowledge is a strategic asset and source of competitive advantage. They must collect, assimilate, disseminate and utilize knowledge, not accumulate information.
- » Developing networks – Leaders must develop a networking capability across the entire company, creating webs of interaction that link people, information, and technology. This requires great skill in communications, relationship building, conflict management, and team learning.
- » Building alliances – Globally literate leaders know how to link their businesses with the outside world of experts and resources. They leverage key external relationships through alliances, joint ventures, and partnerships with competitors, product developers, distributors, and marketers – all to foster collaborative research, marketing agreements, and joint ventures. These leaders use outsourcing to improve flexibility and create new ideas, and are obsessed with getting suppliers, customers, and employees to work together.

MAKING THE IMPOSSIBLE POSSIBLE

The global value network can do things that were previously thought to be either impossible or at least impractical. An importer in Singapore needs approvals from 18 agencies that handle customers and trade approvals in order for a large shipment to move globally. The trader logs on to TradeNet, an Internet-based system developed by the Singapore Trade Development Board, enters its request, and completes the forms online. The forms are instantaneously routed through the 18 different agencies – simultaneously. This whole permitting process is accomplished online in about a quarter of an hour! Globalization and the value network strikes again.[8]

That these complex partnership networks are now being recognized in their totality is, in a way, comforting. Horror movies portray the large, multi-tentacled menaces from the depths of the ocean. We are frightened until we finally see them and realize that this is just a "big, tangled up critter" which grew too big for its environment! Something about human nature prefers the known to the unknown, the named to the nameless – and having partners to being alone.

That this value network of the millennium we call the twenty-first century is complex is not the challenge. That has always been so. That nearly all of it involves partnerships is not surprising either. The challenge is the dynamic, turbulent, unpredictable, and accelerating rate at which all of these elements are changing. *Start by accepting its existence. Then choose partners wisely and begin untangling the complexity – because you don't want your competitors to do it before you.*

HENKEL–MANCO AND WAL-MART

To illustrate a real-world example of a value network under construction, a good example is Manco, the Cleveland (OH) based company, which is part of Henkel's Adhesives Group. When Manco's leader Jack Kahl was considering whether to sell the company to Henkel kGAa (Germany), he was an astute observer of the globalization of his business. Wal-Mart was Manco's largest and most important customer and it was expanding globally on an aggressive scale. Jack was (as usual) competing with the vaunted 3M for a spot on the shelves of Wal-Mart stores – but now these stores were in new places like Brazil, Mexico, Europe, and Asia.

I recall Jack asking his international VP how many people Manco had in Brazil to serve Wal-Mart. The answer (this was a couple of years ago) was "one – part of the time." Then Jack asked how many people 3M had in Brazil (or South America, near Brazil) to serve Wal-Mart. The answer was "around 3000, give or take a few." That was when Jack decided that going it alone in the coming era of global value networks was not going to work. He needed a partner, a big one, and fast. As luck would have it, a mutual friend introduced Jack and Manco to one of the top executives of Henkel, and the rest is history.

In the past few years, Manco's Cleveland-based "Global Business" unit, under the leadership of Jack's son, Bill, has introduced Manco's "Duck®" brand into at least 20 countries. This rapid global rollout has not been easy, but it certainly was accelerated by Manco's "partnership mentality." Bill Kahl and his Manco partners have enlisted help from their Henkel partners in local and regional affiliates in all of these countries. And, as Peter Drucker said in his "Network Society" article, Manco did not just ask, "what do we want to do?" They asked, "what do they want to do?"

Manco and Henkel are now proudly spreading the Duck brand of tapes and adhesives to consumer outlets around the world. Not the least of these are in Wal-Mart stores in (yes) Brazil and in Europe. European retailers are strongly resisting Wal-Mart's invasion of their territory. One of the challenges Henkel faced was if, how, and whether to become a partner to Wal-Mart – or an adversary, by the way of allying with old-line European retailers. To Manco and Henkel's credit, a joint management meeting of their senior executives with those of Wal-Mart found a way to resolve these issues. Henkel wisely decided to serve *both* its loyal, old-line customers and powerful newcomers like Wal-Mart

Will the European retailers who are Henkel's long-time customers like this? I doubt it. But most of them will be realistic enough to understand that a global company of Henkel's size and stature (and Manco's strong ties to Wal-Mart) cannot ignore the potential of the world's largest retailer coming into its backyard.

Wal-Mart has instituted its own form of value network partnerships. It realizes that global expansion of a value network is no simple proposition. Early false steps reinforced Wal-Mart's conclusion that involvement of a key group of partners was essential. This resulted in Wal-Mart relying heavily on a select group of 50 suppliers for global operating insights in addition to being global sourcing partners.

Randy Cameron, Wal-Mart's VP of global sourcing, describes it this way: "The Top 50 multinational strategy is basically partnering with our suppliers on global readiness on how to handle Wal-Mart's growth internationally ... That is different from the function of getting with the rest of the suppliers to source products globally."

> The top 50 are involved more deeply and contribute more input on the directions Wal-Mart is planning, and thus have more control over their own roles as partners.
>
> Once suppliers are selected and terms negotiated, the global sourcing group is responsible for communicating the details of the program to various countries. Not every product or category represents a global opportunity. The decision of what to buy and when to buy is a local decision, but each locale has the option to join with the larger corporate program. These are examples of partnerships at work.

"Companies will need global reach to serve global customers. If they lack the capacity, they must build partnerships around the world. All markets are local markets. Quality, pricing and service must be globally competitive and domestically appropriate. Local distribution will require a much deeper understanding of local business needs and prevailing national cultures."

Robert Rosen[9]

VALUE NETWORK AND GLOBALIZATION

Different countries use different accounting systems and standards. Some have loose, weak, and/or inadequate standards. Governments in some countries meddle in financial disputes. The rules of law so commonly accepted in the United States and Western Europe have a far more structured set of standards than those in developing countries. Just realizing that this is the case is an important part of global knowledge.

These are the kinds of issues the value network and the globalization of partnerships are addressing all around the world. Different countries (even regions) also have very different cultures. Consider the challenges in large, populous countries like India or China that operate under a different set of social rules than Western counterparts.

Even different parts of China operate very differently – the coastal areas and provinces surrounding major cities, especially Hong Kong, operate much more like capitalist partners. Inland, the further one goes, the stranger it can become. The same could be said for the differences in rural and urban cultures in most countries. Europe may standardize on a single currency, but this will not overcome centuries of cultural differences among European countries.

This is truly an important aspect of globalization and of the value network, which can baffle, befuddle, and bedevil prospective partnerships.

NOTES

1 Hamel, Gary (2000) *Leading the Revolution*. Harvard Business School Press, Boston, MA.
2 From an address in Cleveland (OH), and his book, *The Lexus and the Olive Tree*.
3 Remarks made at Cleveland (OH) Council on World Affairs, October 4, (2000).
4 Rosen, Robert (2000) *Global Literacies*. Simon & Schuster, New York.
5 Hamel, ibid.
6 Das, T.K. & Bing-Sheng Teng (1998) "Between trust and control: developing confidence in partner cooperation in alliances." *Academy of Management Review*, Baruch College, CUNY.
7 Rosen, ibid.
8 Boyson, Sandor & Corsi, Thomas (2001) "The real time supply chain", *Supply Chain Management Review*, January–February.
9 Rosen, ibid.

The State of the Art

The state of the art of partnering is discussed in this chapter. Recent ideas are put forth, and there is an in-depth discussion of new and high-performing partnership forms. The means of starting, building, and sustaining partnerships are described, as are the human behavioural aspects of partnerships.

> "Alliances are among people, not just companies ... Alliances live through people – this is how all the parts come together."
>
> *Jordan Lewis*

EMERGENT IDEAS AND CONCEPTS

ConferenceDirect – partnerships built around people

ConferenceDirect (www.conferencedirect.com) is a relatively new company, which is redefining the value creation role of intermediary partners in conference planning and execution. Founded just a few short years ago by former Hilton hotel executives Brian Stevens and Brian Ritchey, ConferenceDirect is growing rapidly, testimony that there is value added by its kind of partnerships with major hotel chains and corporate meeting and conference planners.

As CEO Brian Stevens puts it, "Outsourcing in the US is increasing very rapidly and more people are looking for solutions that are not within their core competencies." As the vertical integration model of business declines, the practice of finding partners who can do what is needed better than the company continues to grow. Stevens says, "we're kind of like Schwab, we can either do it for you or help you get it done yourself."

The key to the success of ConferenceDirect is people-partnerships. Its strength lies in its cadre of experienced and well-connected people it recruited mostly from the hotel industry. Stevens explains it well:

> "No matter how experienced a corporate meeting planner is, s/he hasn't worked the back of the hotel and can't understand that part as well as we do. The hotels realize that too. We start by marketing to people who know us, and trust us, and we ask how we can help them."

A second key feature is that its expansion has put key ConferenceDirect offices/people in most of the major markets where large conferences are held. ConferenceDirect's people are knowledgeable in the business and known by either the meeting planners or the hotel management – or both. Finally, ConferenceDirect's often subtle but highly effective partnerships are funded by the host hotels, and at 10%, the cost is low enough to be more than worth the price for the benefits gained.

Stevens' example is an apt one: "If you want someone to help you buy a good car, why not hire a mechanic, especially if the car dealer will pay for him?"

Most corporate conference planners are overworked and underpaid. A few are seasoned pros, but many are not, seeing the job as a stepping stone on their way to bigger and better things. To make matters worse, busy corporate executives want well-organized, productive, and enjoyable conferences, but don't want to spend much money or time providing guidance and specifications to their own company planners. It is here that a seasoned, experienced partner – one like ConferenceDirect – is so valuable. When meeting planners do their work well, they almost become invisible because the meeting comes off exactly as desired, and all the attention can be on content and attendee satisfaction. That is where ConferenceDirect excels at supporting its partners.

As its literature "sells" it, this is a full service, one-stop-shopping supplier-partner!

THERE'S NO SUBSTITUTE FOR EXPERIENCE[1]

Your meetings are too important for second-guessing. When you work with ConferenceDirect, you'll enjoy peace of mind that comes from partnering with highly seasoned professionals who arrange meetings for many of the nation's most prominent – and demanding – organizations. With an average of at least 10 years of hotel and meeting planning experience, ConferenceDirect associates combine uncompromising attention to detail with creative, results-oriented approaches to achieving your meeting and event objectives.

ONE CALL, YOU SAVE – BOTH TIME AND MONEY[2]

Looking for that perfect venue for your next event, but don't have time to contact and follow up with dozens of different hotels? Call ConferenceDirect. Our associates are in constant contact with

> hundreds of hotels and resorts, so they can quickly find the best possible venue. Best of all, because we are compensated by the hotels directly, there's typically no cost to you. ConferenceDirect will reserve space and negotiate rates on your behalf. To ensure the complete success of your event, we also offer a wide range of fee-based Conference Management services:
>
> 1. Managing on-site logistics of your meeting
> 2. Arranging just the right speakers
> 3. Coordinating destination management details, such as ground transportation, entertainment, activities and more
> 4. Supervising attendee registration and housing
> 5. Negotiating group airfares
> 6. Arranging temporary meeting planning assistance through our strategic business alliances

The function ConferenceDirect performs is not new. Such intermediaries have been around before, but never with the breadth of coverage and depth of talent that ConferenceDirect employs. How well it is getting the job done, and how fast it is growing is testimony to the success of its founders. The idea – attract the best people with the best relationships – is an ideal basis for building partnerships. After all, most partnerships begin (or end) in relationships between people. By picking the top people and using corporate breadth and depth to leverage its relationships with prospective meeting planners, clients, hotels, etc., ConferenceDirect is building partnerships on the strongest of foundations – a people-to-people relationship. Only after these initial people-to-people connections are made, can the company-to-company partnerships progress.

ConferenceDirect practices partnership principles with its own people, who largely work in an "independent contractor model," operating under the umbrella of a corporate "franchise." These people are self-motivated and have the same motivation as the company – to help clients and build their base of contacts and volume. Their incentive is provided in the form of the compensation for the work they bring in, and overhead is kept low, since most of them work from their home offices.

> "An alliance or partnership isn't really a relationship between companies. It's a relationship between specific individuals. When you're talking about strategic alliances of any kind, the only time the company matters is in the status associated with it. But ultimately, you're really talking about people. Whoever is interfacing with the other company, they are the company."
> *Leonard Greenhalgh, professor and author*

Its rapid growth and blue-chip customer list, which includes companies like Microsoft, McDonald's, Morgan Stanley, Roche Laboratories, and Sprint, is testimony to the success of the ConferenceDirect partnership model.

A PARTNERSHIP THAT BENEFITS BABIES

A rather unusual set of partnerships is one that benefits newborn babies in the Columbus (OH) area. It is an alliance between Children's Hospital, a dedicated pediatric hospital, and several other area hospitals.

Mitchell Truax was born six weeks prematurely, and was admitted for seven days to the neonatal intensive-care unit at Riverside Methodist Hospital. He was, at first, unable to eat and breathe at the same time. Five months later, Mitchell is a happy, healthy boy, but for a time, he needed intravenous and other supplemental feeding. But what is so unusual about this?

What is unusual is that Mitchell was born at Riverside Hospital, the state's leader in maternity services, with over 7000 deliveries each year, and cared for in an intensive-care unit located in Riverside, but managed and operated by Children's Hospital, the leading pediatric hospital in the region.

At a time when health care organizations are looking for ways to better utilize resources and stretch finances without eroding care, this partnership is a unique and superb solution. Children's Hospital is now operating such newborn intensive-care units at two other Ohio Health-owned facilities in Columbus, as well as newborn care units at Grant Medical Center and Doctors West. Another unit is also planned for a more limited partnership with Mount Carmel East.

Why would traditional competitors choose to collaborate as partners in such a different and unprecedented manner? The answers are financial and strategic. It makes sense financially, although the hospitals don't share exact figures. It makes even better sense strategically. This way each hospital can have a top-level neonatal unit without the expense of developing it and managing it.

Ancillary benefits are that the need to transfer patients between hospitals is reduced, and control of where care is provided is improved. The partnership also improves the ability of the hospitals to limit the entry of competing medical care companies because a full range of services are already in place. Children's chief executive, Dr Thomas Hansen, sought the partnerships, and still believes "This is the future for us. This is a model aimed at generating best practices that could well work in other cities."

The medical community has been among the slowest to innovate in the business best practices common in factories and multi-unit companies. The standard concern has cited the tradeoff between cost/efficiency and quality of health care. Perhaps success stories like this will encourage doctors and administrators alike to search for the model partnership – a win–win one in which no compromises are necessary!

DELL STILL DOES IT BEST

Many would debate that in the year 2002, Dell Computer is an overused and too-well-known example, but I say this is not so. Much has been written about Dell and to that extent it is overexposed. Not all that much has been written about it from the perspective of partnerships.

Michael Dell and his organization reinvented supply chain management for making PCs. Now Dell is taking that step up the ladder to making servers – which are just larger forms of PCs. The principles Dell uses are similar to those called "Lean Production" in the famed Toyota Production System. Dell has gone a giant step further by attracting chief information officer (CIO) Randy Mott to join it after 20 years at Wal-Mart, the last six as CIO. In doing so, Dell has gained a deep knowledge and understanding of how the leader in the volatile retail industry manages inventory and logistics systems.

Wring the waste out of the supply chain! Shorten the lead times for everything and get connected digitally to customers and suppliers. Run to order instead of to stock! Don't build products far in advance when component costs are declining several percentage points every month. Keep inventory turning, not sitting! Mott says it well:

> "From the time we start with the bare chassis to having a completed PC is generally less than an hour. The next step – a major point of difference compared to our competitors – is to load the software you want to use. For business customers [partners] we've worked with, we actually load their standard configuration exactly the way they want it set up. All of this happens as part of the normal process so there are not any exception steps that add cost."

That is being close to the customer/partner – figuratively and literally.

What is a key element of this strategy? The answer is partnerships with suppliers. Lean production teaches that tightly linked relationships with suppliers are essential. Dell's model proves it! Dell VP Dick Hunter describes it this way:

> "Michael [Dell] focuses relentlessly on driving low-cost material from the supplier through the supply chain to our customers. ... The low cost producer will be the ultimate winner, and that's reflected in Dell's steadily rising market share."

Why does Dell partner with suppliers? Material costs account for 74% of Dell's revenues. That makes supplier relations a large success factor. Dell carries about five days of inventory. That is about 70 turns per year. Compaq claims it is gaining, citing a 60-turn figure, but facts say it is at about 30 turns, and Dell isn't standing still.

> "Partnering on the current scale wouldn't work were it not for the Internet, which can connect the joint venture with its parents in a nearly seamless web."
>
> *James W. Michaels, FORBES.COM*

Dell implemented i2's software at all its global manufacturing sites in 2000, making planning and timely information accessible worldwide. Every line in every factory is scheduled every two hours, and a typical factory runs with five–six hours of inventory including work in process. Reliance on suppliers in this kind of environment is essential, critical, and imperative. Anything but good supplier relations makes such a fast-moving operation perilous or impossible.

Dell's top 30 suppliers provide about 75% of its material cost. Raise that to the top 50 suppliers and the percentage goes to almost 95%. Getting "machine to machine" connection with suppliers, similar to what it has internally, is one of Dell's near-term goals. Making sure its suppliers understand its business model and supply chain management process is a critical part of the partnership.

And Dell doesn't shift suppliers constantly. Only two–three top suppliers have changed in the past three years according to VP Hunter. He says it clearly: "Our goal is to replace inventory with information. The more information we get to our suppliers quickly, the faster we build product, the faster we receive material from suppliers." Every Dell supplier can view its order information via the Web, including long term (4–12 week) planning information all the way down to the two-hour execution systems, which generate the automatic requests for replenishment.

Maybe this is an overused model, but until your company gets to this level of cooperation between plants and suppliers, it is still one of the best to emulate. And for those of you hoping to overtake Dell, here is Mott's closing comment: "I would tell you that there's not anything we're doing in any part of the supply chain that we don't believe we can do better!"

> "In our experience, few executives have more than a superficial understanding of what drives the economic and competitive consequences of strategic alliances."
>
> *Yves Doz and Gary Hamel*

WHERE PARTNERSHIPS START, AND HOW THEY ARE SUSTAINED

How to initiate partnerships and alliances

Where to start, what to do? OK, by now you are sick of hearing about all the kinds of partnerships and alliances and all the reasons they are great or terrible, work or fail. You want to know how to get started, and what to do – right?

THE STATE OF THE ART

Choose a kind of partnership (who)
The place to get started is to *identify a need*. Consider the types of partnerships – with customers, suppliers, employees, and special partners. Then look at the categories for partnerships – marketing and/or customer access, technology and/or proprietary know-how, capacity and/or resources, skills and/or talent, financial and/or economic, and special situations.

Choosing one of these "types" or "categories" is a good place to start. But choose carefully, because success is dependent on making a good choice. Then enlist support from senior management, unless *you are* senior management, and then get support (and accurate feedback) from the working levels, which know a lot more about what really happens in the business.

Many great partnerships start at the VP or director level. People in these positions are high enough to have access to and influence with top management and yet have a realistic perspective of what really goes on at the working level. Starting partnerships at the CEO level is risky because the people feel compelled to go along but may not really believe in the partnerships. They may just be doing it "to please the boss," which is not a good enough reason.

Where to start – organizationally
Starting partnerships lower in an organization – say at the buyer–seller level – is possible but harder. These levels are driven for short-term results and usually spend most of their time in a negotiating "tug-of-war" over details of the deals. Often the ideas for the partnership can originate from strong relationships that people at this level build by working cooperatively over long periods of time.

But getting the managerial support for such "bottom-up" partnerships is not always as easy as it should be. Why? Because someone at higher managerial levels in one of the two organizations will be suspicious or fear that this is just another negotiating ploy.

Establishing a multi-level partnership
As the partnership progresses, more and more of the dealings will be directly between corresponding functional departments in the partner companies (and not always through the purchasing–sales interface). Culture and language barriers and issues must be proactively addressed.

Once this is done, the partnership can proceed to work on the business issues.

Building a partnership on a multi-level organizational basis is the key to both supplier partnerships and customer partnerships, although the multi-level people and respective contact points change depending on which type of partnership it is. Multi-level partnerships can also span another level backward into the supply chain and follow exactly the same process. Build involvement at different organizational levels, but start high enough to assure solid support until trust is developed.

There must be some sort of top executive partnering (at the VP, president, COO, or CEO level) to assure that the entire organizations of both partners recognize the resources, support, and commitment that comes from that level. These should involve face-to-face meetings at least twice a year (more or less depending on the maturity and progress of the relationship). These should be "home and home" meetings, held at alternating sites of each partner. Where the distance or cost of transportation is an obstacle, advanced telecommunications such as video-conferencing can help immensely.

Do not forget to schedule meetings with consideration for the partner's time zone and normal workday! Many a horror story has been told about Japanese top executives who insisted on calling their US managers at 2 a.m. In the US, many Californians must rise before dawn to "attend" a teleconference thoughtlessly scheduled by East Coast counterparts for 8 a.m. – Eastern Time!

The partnership meetings

The partnership meetings must have both private and "public" phases. In the private part, top executives meet alone to openly share their perspectives on how things are going and raise (or resolve) potentially disruptive issues. This part of the meeting can be held before or after the "public" part. In large, strategically critical partnerships, it may be advisable to split the top executive part into two sessions, one before and one after the main (public) partnership meeting.

The open or "public" part of the meeting involves the functional team members from both partners and focuses on a jointly developed agenda of topics. Minutes from prior meetings (if this is not the first meeting) including progress on agreed actions, are distributed in advance and reviewed for results and obstacles (so top management can collaborate to remove the obstacles). New opportunities for improvement should be identified, brainstormed, and then moved to the "to do" list – or put on hold for discussion at a future meeting. Difficult issues or problems, such as failings in quality or service by the supplier, poor forecasting, inadequate lead times, or insufficient communication/information from the customer, are all fair game for this discussion.

The irritants to be dealt with

Refer to the "irritants" list below for a listing of potential problem causes. Someone at a fairly high level (VP of the host partner) should lead this meeting and keep it on track and on agenda. In partnerships that are moving along well, it is ideal to hold a more relaxed "social" event on the evening preceding the actual meeting (a dinner or reception) to allow personal acquaintances to be made and renewed up, down, and across both organizations. Many people in top management never meet the working-level people (even in their own companies) in this sort of setting. The importance of this type of event should not be minimized – it sets the stage for cooperative relations during the partnership meeting.

There are many other dimensions to this multi-level meeting. Some of these are covered elsewhere as they come up. Rather than try to cover too many nuances here, I want to review a couple of other kinds of partnership meetings that have proven effective. There are at least two that warrant specific mention: the *business (team) partner meeting* and the *functional partner meeting*. These team meetings are essential to the customer partnership as well.

The business partner meeting consists of mid- to lower-level working management in the functions that do the primary buying or selling and implementation of the agreed-upon purchases and sales. This is the closest meeting to the old buy–sell relationship. The meeting and relationship at this level are really where the "heart and soul" of the partnership live.

The functional partner meeting consists of people who have mirror image functions in the partner companies. Examples of these meeting participants are those responsible for shipping and receiving, accounts payable and receivable, engineering and quality, and so forth. Getting these people together takes issue resolution out of the realm of negotiation and into the realm of partnering for the best results.

The key irritants from the customer's viewpoint are:[3]

- » Stock-outs and late or poor delivery.
- » Back orders and long reorder cycles.
- » Inadequate communication or poor information.
- » Confusing or rapidly changing terms and allowances.
- » Unrelated or unclear marketing campaigns.
- » Frequent personnel changes in sales representatives or account managers.
- » Incomplete or poorly thought-out promotions and plans.
- » Inadequate lead times on promotion plans.
- » Inaccessibility to supplier management.
- » Inexplicable policies (at least by the sales representatives).
- » Billing disagreements.
- » New product introductions or major product line changes with too little advance notice.
- » Decentralized and often autonomous multi-division structures where several sales representatives from the same company sell closely related but different products to the same buyer, with differing terms, programs, and so on.

The key irritants from the supplier's viewpoint are:

- » Confusing or complicated scheduling of appointments and meetings with buyers.
- » Buying decisions attributed to anonymous sources such as "the committee" or simply "they."
- » Execution of delivery, setup, display, or promotion different from what was agreed upon.
- » Sudden changes in inventory needs – cutbacks or cancellations or unexpected surges in demand – with little or no advance notice.
- » Failure to keep planned meeting schedules or delaying meetings inexplicably for hours.
- » Sudden or major strategic direction changes.

- » Last-minute cancellation of promotions that had been organized at great expense and for which inventory has already been committed.
- » Frequent buying staff changes or changes in the mix of assigned duties.
- » Inaccessible senior management.
- » Billing disputes and deductions.

"Trying to create a competency your company lacks is costly, time consuming and often doomed to failure. Buying them via M & A is expensive and tricky. Partnering is the cheapest and safest way: no dilution, no dangerous leveraging of the balance sheet. If the deal doesn't work, dissolve it."

James W. Michaels, editor emeritus, FORBES.COM

What is collaboration?

All partnerships depend on collaboration between people – between members of both partner organizations. Many people would say such collaboration is teamwork, and that is close, but not quite right. Teamwork has become an overworked word in the past two decades. Teamwork is not always collaboration – although collaboration is usually good teamwork.

A recent buzzword is "collaborative commerce," but this term is of limited use. Agile Software Corp. CEO Bryan Stolle chuckles as he says, "Collaboration is almost a meaningless term that is grossly overused. What isn't collaborative? Everything you do on the Internet is collaborative. It can mean anything." The challenge in making these kinds of partnerships work is to make the collaboration a reality. Len Prokopets, a senior manager at Deloitte Consultants, echoes this when he says, "Now the emphasis is on building a consensus among suppliers and trading partners about the best ways to integrate all of the processes that go into making e-commerce happen." Regardless of the buzzwords used, the important point is that partnerships work and collaboration is what makes them work.

All partnerships are, in varying degrees, some kind of collaborative effort. There must be other fundamentals: well-thought-out strategy, attention to execution, plenty of communication, and, of course, trust. Some partnerships are lousy ones; some are great ones; and most fall somewhere in the middle. That is why learning about how to collaborate effectively will make you "smart" about building better partnerships.

> "It's easy to get good players. Getting 'em to play together effectively, that's the hard part."
> *Casey Stengel, manager, New York Yankees*

SUCCEEDING TOGETHER IS FUN AND DEPENDS ON PEOPLE

Did you ever notice that society places a premium on people who get things done? They usually get paid more, get promoted more often, generally seem to be better liked, and they are also more energized by their work and life overall. People who get things done are often the most active volunteer leaders in church and community organizations too. Why?

Because they seem to know *how* to get things done! Mind you, these people don't do it all themselves – they find partners who help them. They may do very little of what it is that needs to get done. What they do very well is to get other people to cooperate with them and help them get things done. What they do even better is to get people to collaborate with them in doing so.

> "We long to participate in a meaningful workplace where we are appreciated for our contributions."
> *Stephen M. Dent*

Cooperation is a more passive "I'll go along with you and help with that" attitude. Collaboration is a more active "Let me help you with that, because I know another, better way to do it" mindset. When you set out to do something, you're limited by your own knowledge and abilities (and physical resources too!). When a group sets out to do the same thing and the members partner to cooperate with each other, the task usually gets done faster and more easily. When the members of that group decide to really put their minds together and collaborate on getting the job done, it gets done more effectively, too.

"Participative management is not democratic. Having a say differs from having a vote."

Max DePree

Use collective knowledge

The best way to capitalize on opportunities is by using the collective knowledge of a group of people collaborating. You may mistakenly think you have to operate alone. You don't - in fact, far from it. You may think that passive or active cooperation is enough, but it isn't - if you want the best outcome. Collaborating means that you bring your knowledge and contribute this knowledge openly and freely. In partnering efforts, teamwork and collaboration often get confused.

"Partnerships may be a necessity, but teamwork is tough. And that's a lesson that many are about to find out the hard way."

James Daly

Learn about behavior – Maslow and McGregor

Abraham Maslow is still right. Douglas McGregor was too. Who are these two guys? They are two men who studied why people behave in certain ways. What they found was that people behave in certain ways because of feelings, beliefs, and values they have developed in their lives and situations in which they live and work. The motivation of people is the topic of hundreds of books, but the work of two people is important because their work helps explain why people behave the way they do - in business, in life, and in collaborative partnerships. To succeed in collaboration, partnerships, and with people working together, it is important to understand what motivates people to behave the way they do.

Douglas McGregor attempted to categorize the motivation of people into two, rather simplistic, but actually quite profound, types. He called them Theory X and Theory Y. There has since been a Theory Z developed, but that one comes closer to self-motivation and relates more to Maslow's works. If you want more information on McGregor's theories, you can read his classic book titled *The Human Side of Enterprise* (McGraw-Hill, 1985 reprint). Here are his basic theories.

Theory X:

"The average human being has an inherent dislike of work and will avoid it if he can ... and prefers to be directed, wishes to avoid responsibility, has little ambition and wants security above all. Most people must be coerced, directed and threatened with punishment."

Theory Y:

"... physical and mental effort in work is as natural as play or rest ... External control and threat of punishment are not the only means for bringing about effort toward organizational objectives. The average human being learns, under proper conditions, not only to accept but to seek responsibility."

Maslow's brilliant original book on human motivation had such an unusual title (*Eupsychian Management*) that it attracted little attention. Fortunately, it has now been reissued with additional commentary under the title *Maslow on Management* (Wiley, 1998). The centerpiece of Maslow's principles was a pyramid-shaped hierarchy of needs which motivate human behavior (Fig. 6.1). If you remember these, you will understand why people involved in collaboration or partnerships behave the way they do.

"The musician must make music, an artist must paint, a poet must write, if he is to ultimately be at peace with himself. What a man can be, he must be."

Abraham Maslow

Partnerships and quality management

Another useful way to look at partnerships is provided by Stephen Dent in his book *Partnering Intelligence* (Davies-Black, 1999). It draws from the Shewhart PDCA process of problem analysis and solution used by many quality and TQM disciplines and made famous by quality guru W. Edwards Deming. Dent adds the sociologist's perspective with the team formation stages of forming – storming – norming – performing.

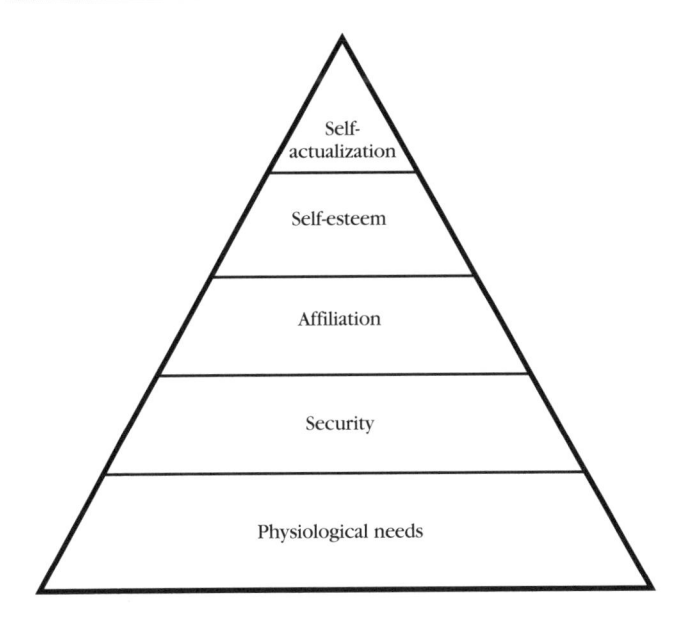

Fig. 6.1 Maslow's hierarchy of needs.

Essentially, what Dent is saying is that partnerships don't exist only at one extreme or the other – "wonderful or awful" – but at all levels of human interaction, on a continuum. When you are discouraged by the wide variation of partnership development and success in your company or organization it will be helpful to remember that this is not a black or white situation. It is all shades of gray – good and bad alike!

Dent further introduces a comprehensive set of diagnostic tools to assess just how good a partner you would be, and how good a partner's prospects would be (Fig. 6.2). I may oversimplify it badly, but in essence partnership is a lot like friendship: "To have a friend, you must be a friend; to have a partner, you must be a partner!" If you can only remember that phrase, you will have gained a valuable piece of insight!

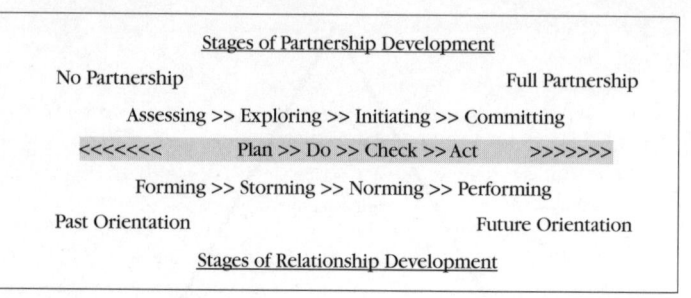

```
              Stages of Partnership Development
   No Partnership                                    Full Partnership
           Assessing >> Exploring >> Initiating >> Committing
       <<<<<<<         Plan >> Do >> Check >> Act      >>>>>>>
           Forming >> Storming >> Norming >> Performing
   Past Orientation                                 Future Orientation
              Stages of Relationship Development
```

Fig. 6.2 The partnership continuum model (Stephen M. Dent (1999) *Partnering Intelligence*. Davies-Black, Palo Alto, CA, reprinted with permission).

A prescription for the future

Bud LaLonde is professor emeritus of logistics from Ohio State University. He offers a refreshing perspective on the future including three guideposts for the future. LaLonde poses a challenging question (and then answers it):

> "What if there is no tomorrow in terms if technology fixes, or the prospects for resources turn dismal? Will there be a tendency to consign to the scrap heap most of the effort devoted to building the supply chain? When things get tough, are all bets off and will all of the supply chain partners head for the nearest foxhole?"

Considering that the US economy at this time is nearing the first recession in over a decade, this is a good time to pose such a question. Shortsighted, powerful buyers are brutalizing partners into unfair deals – essentially reaching into their partners' pockets to take money out of them. This happens when there is a tough economic time, and weaker buyers resort to old-fashioned, power-based bargaining. These tactics do great harm to partnerships, harm that is often irreparable. But as the old saying says, "what comes around, goes around." Time will change and things will even out.

LaLonde provides three guideposts to use in the tough times to make sure a company makes it through them in the right way.[4]

- **Guidepost 1 - Education**. Educate the generation of managers who have not had the challenge of managing through turbulent times. They need to understand the organization's core competencies, and the internal and external relationships that need to be protected.
- **Guidepost 2 - Partnerships**. Over the next few years, managers will have an opportunity to ascertain who their supply chain partners really are. It's relatively easy to be a partner in good times. The real test is making a supply chain partnership work when times are not so good.
- **Guidepost 3 - Decision making**. Companies will be required to learn how to make technology decisions on the basis of "need to have" not "nice to have." Knowing the difference might be the key to survival.

All I can say is "so true." Partners must stick together in good times and bad ones. To do that, people must understand what role the partners play and how to productively use technology to support the partnership - not to undermine it.

NOTES

1 ConferenceDirect promotional brochure.
2 Ibid.
3 Mariotti, John L. (1996) *The Power of Partnerships*, Blackwell, Oxford.
4 LaLonde, Bud (2001) "Guideposts for turbulent times." *Supply Chain Management Review*, March–April.

In Practice

Several case studies of organizations are included in this chapter. The cases describe philosophical, global, and cultural challenges of making partnerships work, and describe some errors that can lead to failure.

PARTNERSHIP PHILOSOPHY COUNTERS "PURCHASING PARANOIA"

Amrep is a medium-sized company based in Marietta (GA) just outside of Atlanta. Amrep is a specialty chemical formulator and packager of aerosols, liquids, lubricants, and other similar products. Most people either use or come in contact with Amrep's products constantly. Its cleaning products are used in institutional and industrial applications of all kinds. Its automotive chemicals, many of them in aerosol cans, appear on the shelves of the leading US auto retailers, companies like AutoZone, Advanced Auto, and many others. Its consumer products show up in many leading retail shops. Because many of the products are "private labeled," Amrep isn't a household name, even though it's "Misty" brand does large volume in itself.

Under the leadership of CEO Kevin Gallagher, Amrep has increased in size by over three times in the past 10 years. There are many reasons for this increase, but one that Gallagher puts high on the list is partnership – both with suppliers and with customers. The philosophy that Gallagher leads by is one which treats suppliers like partners and reaps the rewards of being treated that way in return.

This philosophy developed after Gallagher spent years working for larger corporations seeing the insular, paranoid behavior that limited their success. He found it common for adjacent areas to know little about what each other was doing. The purchasing department was paranoid about letting suppliers into the company – figuratively and literally.

When he was hired to turn around SNE Enterprises, the producer of Crestline windows, Duo-Temp storm doors, and a line of other branded window and door products, he decided to break that mold and include suppliers instead of exclude them. He created the philosophy of integrating "vendors" as "partners" – as he puts it, "from cradle to grave, raw material to finished sale, and beyond." He expanded that partnership philosophy when he purchased Amrep with the intention of building it into a leading company in a badly fragmented industry.

One of the events that not only symbolized the partnership but also solidified it was the "Vendor Appreciation Day" that was originated to recognize superior-performing vendor-partners. During this daylong event, Amrep informs, recognizes, and entertains its supplier partners, holding morning meetings, an afternoon golf outing, and an evening awards banquet and ceremony. As an unusual twist, Gallagher held a separate "private/special" business review session at this event for those vendor-partners who sent senior executives to attend it. Many small, private companies guard their financial results fiercely and often don't even share them with their own management. In holding that special session, he broke with tradition and shared the in-depth financial information about the company's performance with the vendor executives. The condition for getting the "inside scoop" was for senior management to attend the "Vendor Appreciation Day."

The typical attendees at such meetings are sales reps, sales managers, and an occasional regional sales exec. This entire group would hear the company highlights at a larger session during the evening meeting. But as word of this "private session" spread, more executives began to attend, and confidence with the company grew. In later meetings, as many as 10 or more executives of billion-dollar corporate suppliers attended the "Vendor Appreciation Day" and the "special meeting." Since open sharing of information is a huge trust builder, this move complemented the partnership philosophy. Since the top management was now privy to the financial performance, the supplier companies could be more comfortable extending financing/terms and, in doing so, help fuel growth for both partners.

Many companies have vendor meetings, and most give awards to high-performing suppliers of materials that go into their products. Gallagher expanded the awards to include key providers of professional, administrative, and transportation services and many others. Moreover, the philosophy permeated the meeting and the "Partner of the Year" awards ceremony. Not only are the typical functions enjoyed, but also there is a chance for suppliers to meet and get to know a broad group of company management – not just the sales–purchasing contact that is so often the norm.

The partnership feeling becomes tangible as both partners act like partners – talking to each other, as partners would – not as adversaries. The openness and sharing create a sense of trust, and as the relationship is built, there is a sense of intimacy that is often missing. Of course, there are a few "so-called" partners who come out of the meetings and spread gossip or divulge confidential information. These are fairly quickly identified, and eliminated from the group (and usually from the supplier position, too!).

Suppliers who are accustomed to doing the entertaining are entertained – and at Amrep's expense. Suppliers are also asked to not entertain Amrep purchasing people in the course of the business relationship (a policy position Amrep shares with retail giant Wal-Mart, among others). Kevin Gallagher's language as he describes this partnership reveals how his leadership philosophy helps reinforce it: "They talk to us as a partner and not as a salesman. They act the way you treat them."

As the partnerships grow, supplier partners have access to Amrep plants where they might help solve problems, try out new ideas, prove new technology or processes, and much more. One of Amrep's largest suppliers frequently steers it to new sales opportunities in related products – because it knows that a win-win opportunity is good for both partners. Another large supplier's chief financial officer (CFO) receives monthly financial reports, building trust and confidence while providing valuable management advice to Amrep. Occasionally, when a supplier partner needs "help" in the form of sales volume a little earlier than the normal demand, arrangements are made to accommodate a special order, thus meeting the needs of both partners. Over time, the partnership philosophy with suppliers infects the sales organization and it takes a similar approach with customers – open, positive, a believer in partnerships.

Spin-offs of this partnership philosophy include a "Hall of Fame" which features *individuals*, people from supplier partners who are recognized for their contribution to the partnership. This is entirely consistent with the important point that partnerships begin and grow with people. Kevin Gallagher sums it up well when talking about partnerships that spill over from suppliers to customers: "The partner understands what value you're bringing to the partnership because it is in front of them all the time." That's a partnership philosophy that works!

Key partnership principles make this example so rich: sharing information, building trust, spreading the partnership across the

> organization from top to bottom, and finding win-win deals. Those are ingredients that make partnerships work.

AIRLINES' UNEASY ALLIANCES

One of the largest, most global, and tenuous alliances is that of "code-sharing" alliances between major airlines. I use it as an example because it encompasses the right reasons for forming partnerships and alliances, but it also shows the perils of such partnerships.

In *The Lexus and the Olive Tree*, Thomas Friedman frames the issue aptly:

> "We have moved from a world where everyone wants to go it alone – where the rugged individualist is the executive role model and the vertically integrated company that does it all is the corporate model – to a world where you can't survive unless you have lots of allies, where the Churchillian alliance maker is the executive role model and the horizontally allied company is the corporate model."

Whew! In that one sentence of 67 words, Friedman explains why the large airlines are partnering more and more.

In global economies, no company is large enough or powerful enough to reach across all markets – and if it was, its sheer capital intensity and infrastructure size would be a challenge to manage. Airlines have been notable for their difficulty making money, and especially making a return on capital – in good times or bad ones.

Add to this the complexity of nationalistic cultures, rules, regulations, and local pride, and the airlines are better off partnering than expanding globally. Thus the formation of several huge alliances occurs. The Star Alliance encompasses (among others, because change often occurs faster than books can be updated) United (United States), Air Canada (Canada), SAS (Europe), Varig (Europe), Lufthansa (Europe) and Thai Airways (Asia). The symbolic picture showing an elongated plane carrying these logos conveys the visual imagery quite well. The motto completes the job: *"Star Alliance – The Airline Network for Earth."*

Making the partnership work is quite another matter. Unpublicized "tugs-of-war" abound, about schedules, flight designations, fare bases, shared facilities, shared equipment, shared people, rules, and many other practices. Prospective or rumored mergers send tremors through the various partners. And yet, such partnerships may be the best, or only, feasible solution to creating a global airline without the investment and risk needed to do so. Just remember the importance of balanced risks and rewards. Recall the need for open information sharing and communications. Add the need for trust, and you see the challenge.

Even so, in response to the Star Alliance, US mega-airline American Airlines led the formation of "One World," a comparable global airline partnership encompassing a handful of major airlines. Its motto hammers home the rationale: *"One World – Now you can look forward to recognition on seven of the world's finest airlines."* Delta Airlines was forced to form alliances with Alitalia and Air France or face the prospect of "strategic isolation."

The one reason, perhaps the only one, that these kinds of partnerships work is that they are truly alliances not partnerships. The companies keep their own identities within the alliance. They agree to work together because it is mutually beneficial and better than all the other options.

> Expect more global alliances for the same reasons. Some will lead to mergers, others to close partnerships, many more will fall apart. Nonetheless, partnerships and alliances are an increasing response to the demands of globalization. And also remember that whoever chooses and keeps the best partners wins!

CANON – APPEAL TO HIGHER PURPOSE – KYOSEI[1]

Canon's honorary chairman of the board, Ryuzaboro Kaku, has instilled in that company a clear philosophy that endures. His vision of the future is "Living and working for the common good." Using the Japanese concept of *Kyosei*, which means "symbiosis," Canon has taken the philosophy of partnerships and alliances to a new level.

Kyosei is a universal principle, but Canon's central business strategy is based on two main goals – wealth creation and distribution – but within a framework of living together and working for the common good. Kyosei promotes harmonious relations with owners, customers, suppliers, the natural environment, and even competitors. When a group of companies use Kyosei, it becomes a powerful force for social, political, and economic transformation.

By using Kyosei, companies find new ways of doing business, and new approaches to the business strategy, organizational forms, and management practices. Canon uses five stages in making Kyosei work for it.

» Stage 1 – Commit yourself to economic survival. A company's first responsibility is economic survival, but this is just the beginning.
» Stage 2 – Create partnerships with people. A company must share its future prosperity with its workers, such that each employee makes Kyosei a part of his/her personal belief system.
» Stage 3 – Create partnerships with outside stakeholders. Internal partnerships are not enough. Customers and suppliers who are treated well respond in the same way, giving back loyalty. Higher profits for all partners are the goal. Such partnerships are even extended to competitors like Hewlett Packard, Kodak, and Texas Instruments. "A rising tide lifts all ships" is the premise.
» Stage 4 – Assume global social responsibility, and take responsibility for cooperation with foreign companies and foreign countries. Build facilities in regions that have a trade imbalance, and train local workers to sustain the investment.
» Stage 5 – Be active globally, making government a Kyosei partner and working to improve conditions like environmental quality.

Kaku sees Kyosei as the platform for continued success. He realizes that each region of the world will see it slightly differently, but finds that to be expected. Kaku believes that Kyosei is his legacy to ensure that the next generation will understand how to apply it successfully. The evidence thus far – Canon's success – says it is working – just like partnerships work when properly done.

> Partnerships that are based on win-win principles are the most successful and last the longest because it is in everyone's best interest to sustain them. Basing relationships on Kyosei is equivalent to committing to win-win partnerships. This does not mean being soft or easy - it means looking for the common good and finding a way that the partnerships can serve it, even if doing that is tough.

NAVISTAR AND APS – A MODEL PARTNERSHIP

When I write about things based on what has happened around me there is a comfort level that they are (or were) true. Even this is based on my own perspective. In their more lucid moments most managers and executives realize they receive mostly managed information from the organization designed to make them feel good. This "filtered input" has always concerned me. That concern keeps me constantly on the lookout for cases that either reinforce (or contradict) my beliefs. That is where this story came from.

It was a sunny spring day in Knoxville (TN) when I arrived at the modern APS offices. The president of APS and the human resource manager greeted me. Then the fun began. They described how APS is a partner with Navistar (the industrial truck maker) and does much of Navistar's basic accounting work.

As I asked questions and they described how they worked, their vocabulary and signals all pointed to this being the kind of powerful partnership which makes "outsourcing" no longer a dirty word. Companies can only afford to invest in and develop the things that are part of their core competencies.

For many companies, keeping the books and paying or collecting the bills has precious little to do with those competencies. At APS, this is what they do best. Navistar wanted this kind of service and after selecting three smaller cities where it felt costs might be lower, it found Knoxville and APS. APS is a company created specifically to serve Navistar. APS started with around 50 people (please don't call them "temps" because they really aren't).

Navistar sets the "boundaries" of what authority APS has. APS formed teams – self-directed teams – to work within those boundaries. The teams are organized around the kind of work to be done. One team keeps the general ledger. Another pays suppliers. A third pays other bills including travel costs. A series of teams are split by the type of customer, and take care of invoicing. The last team is a general support team.

The offices are physically organized so the teams are together in close proximity. The camaraderie is evident. Some team members are cross-trained to move between jobs and even between teams. There are over 80 people now, and there is no doubt among them who their customer – and partner – is. It is Navistar. There are Navistar employees on site, but the number is down from 12 at the start to just 8 now. The savings to Navistar are millions of dollars per year, directly due to this partnership.

The most successful partnerships are based on choosing good partners to start with. There must be something of comparable value for both partners in the partnership. That is the case here. Open sharing of information is critical. The immediate answer to my question of whether Navistar knew how much profit APS makes was "of course they do."

When I asked about the future, APS cited two simple goals: stay abreast of Navistar's needs, and find another partner/company to create another success for APS. The answer about competition was even refreshing: "We don't focus on competition. We're busy taking care of our customer." I would describe this as a model partnership.

APS get a lot of visitors (like me) to see how it is doing it. The physical surroundings don't tell the story. The attitudes, behavior, and values of the people make the difference. That is a little harder to "see," but it's there if you look closely: small groups of two or three people discussing business in their adjacent cubicles or over the short (4½ft (1.4m)) partitions that separate the team members; eight people doing some "group learning" in front of a TV monitor, easel, and podium in the lunchroom; a busy, but not frantic, work pace in a quiet, "doing the job" atmosphere. Smiles greet the visitors and management. A sidebar conversation occupies the president briefly here and there.

Surprisingly, not all the information came in electronically. There was still a lot of paper shuffling. That just represents another opportunity.

I believe APS will capitalize on it. When APS has really arrived, some of its contacts at Navistar that aren't familiar with it will even stop referring to APS as the "temp agency." APS will be happier when that happens.

How long can such a partnership last? As long as the people involved choose to keep it together. Changing the people changes the dynamics of the relationship, and that can either strengthen or tear apart partnerships. The choice is that of the partners.

The future of the business world holds much uncertainty. Rapid, unpredictable change is one of the few things on which most people can agree. Being good at too many things is neither practical nor profitable. The successful companies of the future will be able to react to change with incredible speed and flexibility by shifting their shape to create and deliver value better than their competitors – by being very good at what they do – and doing just what they are very good at.

The cornerstones of such a rapid "shape-shift" are partnerships with highly competent, closely linked partners. On that sunny spring afternoon, I was able to see a partnership success story right there next to the I-75 and -40 highways. The interstate traffic was starting to back up at 4 p.m., but things were moving smoothly at the Navistar/APS partnership. My beliefs about how partnerships can work were reinforced. That was a good day, and a model partnership.

> Choosing partners carefully and having a clear set of goals and objectives are critical success factors. When the partnership is focused on a single partner's needs, it makes everything else simple and is an excellent way to start making partnerships work. When all of the people in the partnership understand the basis for the partnership, then their efforts are naturally more focused – thus the importance of open communication and sharing of information. Also, hidden agendas can't survive long when this is done!

"Happily mergers and acquisitions aren't the only way to go for companies trying to quicken sluggish growth. Strategic alliances can work as well or better. Never mind the pretentious term – this is nothing more than old-fashioned partnering."

James W. Michaels

CISNEROS GROUP – PARTNERING ON MANY LEVELS[2]

Gustavos Cisneros is a well-connected man, both literally and figuratively. He is one of only seven people from Latin America who appear on the list of the most influential people in the world. As CEO of the powerful media group Cisneros Group of Companies (CGC) he is often compared to people like Rupert Murdoch. Univision is already the largest Spanish-speaking TV network in the United States. CGC recently partnered with AOL, bringing the power of the Internet to 450 million people from Mexico to Chile.

Cisneros believes in using partnerships to multiply the reach of his enterprise. In addition to AOL, CGC has partners like Disney, Motorola, Hearst, Blockbuster, Virgin, and even Playboy. Sometimes these partners find themselves cooperating in one market/venture and competing in another – a common challenge in a global marketplace.

CGC partnerships also reach out to social influences. In conjunction with Microsoft, CGC is developing a satellite-based training program for 1800 teachers in more than 115 primary schools in Latin America. Cisneros himself forms partnerships not just on a personal and corporate level, but also on a national scale. He received Spain's Order of Isabel Las Catolica from King Juan Carlos for strengthening relationships between Spain and Venezuela.

CGC's experiences in Latin America are a lesson for the rest of the world. To stay ahead in this networked world, one of the skills most valuable is know-how in partnering, and the ability to find synergistic potential in partnerships. To do this, CGC must first have the right environment for committed, creative, and loyal employees. Cisneros puts it this way:

> "Partnering is key to our successful international expansion, It means being business-savvy and pragmatic to identify those times when it makes most sense to work with a business partner whose

strength, insight, and experience can complement our credentials. Our challenge is to integrate the cultural differences of our expansive network of business partners."

> When a powerful leader is behind a partnership effort, the chances of success go up astronomically. The more powerful the leader and the stronger his/her conviction, the broader the influence of partnering will spread. The more it spreads, the more proficient the organization becomes at making partnerships work, and then the more it can spread them further.

BP AMOCO PLC – AND CHINA

Mark Graham, cited in *IndustryWeek*, describes a situation that aptly illustrates the range of good and bad news from globalization of the value network:

> "In theory, foreigners can come into China independently, without an obligation to find a local partner, but few do, relying on their joint-venture Chinese contacts to oil the communist bureaucratic wheels and sort the workforce chaff from the wheat."

Graham then goes on to describe one joint-venture example of this principle that worked, and the contrasting setting for many that fail:

> "It is a formula that has worked well for BP Amoco PLC in its far-western venture. The company's $200 million commodity chemical plant in Chongquin [China], built under budget and on time, managed to turn in a $2 million profit during its first year of operation, no mean feat in the boondocks of China."

Just as you might be getting the feeling that these partnership principles in strange cultures are not so mystical, I want to use another quote from Graham's story to dispel that myth:

"Even with government goodwill and financial sweeteners, joint-venture projects are fraught with potential difficulties and misunderstandings. When Mao-suit-wearing cadres meet MBA-degree-wielding managers, something has to give; outsiders are told that they have to get used to the 'Chinese way', which often in reality is the 'socialist way,' characterized by intransigence and xenophobia."[3]

Clearly, the smart thing to know is that among the various parts of the value network and in partnering, the culture match (or conflict) is among the most critical things to understand, deal with, and build upon – or avoid – as the case may be. Even Manco, as a part of global parent Henkel, periodically struggles with the issues of local culture and local autonomy. It is simply difficult for people to put aside long and deeply entrenched beliefs, even if they intend to. Never forget that.

Graham sums it up pretty well, and I'll use his words:

"And therein lies the rub for manufacturers contemplating a pioneering trip into China's Wild West. The journey may be a rough one; partnering two sets of participants with diametrically opposed attitudes and upbringing is never easy."

The same could be said regardless of the geographical countries involved. Check out the cultures – they are critical to global partnership success.

> Making partnerships work across very different cultures is very difficult. Partners must both see the benefits for them and be willing to be flexible to achieve them. There is no such thing as an easy cross-cultural partnership, so when undertaking one, be prepared for challenges and be committed to work through them.

SONY AND AOL

Sony, a Japanese world leader in consumer electronics, is partnering with America Online, the US leader in Web portals. In what seems to be a win-win proposition (for the time being anyway) these two leaders announced a partnership to use Sony's popular PlayStation 2 as an access device to AOL's portal and to jointly develop the software and hardware to let users access the two concurrently.

PlayStation 2 users could both play a game and run popular AOL features like instant messaging, chat, and e-mail. It is not much of an intuitive leap to imagine users both competing and conversing at the same time – much as they would in a real games room.

The synergy between these two companies and their products bodes well for this kind of partnership. There should be substantial benefits in it for both, and the risk/reward and resource balance shouldn't be a problem. In fact, the alliance's largest problem might be Microsoft, which has various agreements and involvement with both of these partners.

Sony's competitor, Nintendo, will also be trying to combat the competitive disadvantage it might find at the hands of Sony-AOL. AOL sees this as an entry to the heavy users of Sony's PlayStation 2 – almost 3 million of them. Sony sees the game-savvy AOL subscribers – 29 million of them – as a rich market for its products. This sounds like a global win-win partnership.

In the direction of partnership types, Sony is taking unprecedented steps in selling one of its Japanese factories to consumer electronics maker Solectron. Solectron's CEO, Koichi Nishimura, is Japanese, and used his Japanese-style passion to convince Sony that it could trust Solectron as its manufacturing partner in a county where *"monozukuri"* – literally "making things" – is a cherished way of life.

For Solectron, "making things" is its foundation, but for a major Japanese consumer electronics company to sell one of its Japanese plants to another, non-Japanese company like Solectron is a landmark event. Sony is one of Japan's most innovative companies, yet its return on equity is low. Factories don't help that situation, and selling factories to trusted partners frees Sony assets to be put to more productive use. Thus the sale of the Nakaniida plant to Solectron.

Sony also uses what it calls "soft alliances" with competitors in other fields. Its music unit teamed with rival Universal Music Group to form Duet, an online music service that makes thousands of songs available to online consumers, and avoids some of the sticky royalty issues that threaten Napster, Sony, and Universal.

Sony's CEO Nobuyuki Idei oversees about 100 partnerships of various kinds. Clearly, Sony is practicing innovation in partnerships, not just in its products.

> When two industry leaders decide to join forces, the power is immense. So are the forces trying to pull them apart. Both are accustomed to being the boss and calling the shots, so the potential benefits must be great enough that they are willing to subordinate some of their desires to make the partnership work. Confidence in the partner's ability to deliver on the promises of the partnership is a key ingredient - it's called "trust!"

WHEN INFORMATION TECHNOLOGY DOESN'T WORK ... A REVERSE CASE STUDY!

Too many case studies focus only on what has worked and how such wonderful results were achieved. Yet, some of the most valuable (albeit painful) learning comes when things don't work. Here is a "generalized" case to help avoid those painful ways of learning, and it has to do with something most companies can relate to - information technology.

When you make an investment in information technology, you are essentially also choosing a partner that you will be working with for a long time - years at least. How well you make this choice, and whether you understand that you are actually choosing a partner and not just a product, is important. There are some things you can ask, some things to look for, and if you do this homework well, your choice will be much more likely to be a good one.

THE NEXT DREAM TEAM – OR ANOTHER CRASH COMING?

One of the most written about and admired joint efforts was the coalition (call it a partnership if you want) between i2, Ariba,

> and IBM. This powerful grouping was supposed to dominate the B2B/e-commerce/supply chain field. Has it? Not even close! Why? Because it wasn't, and perhaps couldn't be, a true partnership. Now Manugistics is combining efforts with Microsoft and KPMG to do the same (or at least a similar) kind of thing. Will this one work? I doubt it. Why? Same problem.
>
> When any of the partners decides that it has the power to compete directly with another partner, the partnership is doomed. These are great partnerships on paper, and offer huge opportunities for synergy, resource sharing, and results. Unfortunately, large powerful companies have a lot of trouble really sharing enough of their power with partners to make partnerships work.

When you buy information technology systems – software or hardware – you will have problems of some kind. You will need help from the supplier's customer support department. It is wise to ask in advance:

» How many people does it have in customer support?
» What is the typical time waiting to speak to one of them?
» How competent and well trained are they?

One of the most devastating situations is to buy an information technology solution from a company that goes out of business. It's really hard to partner with a company that no longer exists! This is not a far-fetched possibility in today's environment. When considering prospective partners, consider these points:

» How financially stable is the prospective supplier?
» Is it privately or publicly owned, and who controls it?
» What assurances and options can you negotiate in the contract in case it is acquired?
» Do you get the rights to the product (code) or some other kind of insurance if it ceases to exist?

What do current customer-partners think of this supplier, its products, and service? Surprisingly many companies don't ask this question nearly often or persistently enough. Get a list of current customers, and *choose* who to call (not the seller – of course it'll give you friendly customers). When you contact them, be sure to consider and/or ask:

» What does the trade press say about this company and product?
» What do current (or former!) customers say about its product, service, and the conversion experience?
» Who can you visit that is using the product to talk to more than a carefully screened few people?
» What products are the companies on the client list actually using now, and for how long?

There is a lot of information out there if you just look for it. A single trip to visit two-three users can be worth its weight in gold – and worth days of internal analysis. Negotiation about the "what-ifs?" when something unfortunate happens is always easier when the purchase/sale is being considered, while the partnership is being formed, rather than after the fact when trouble has started.

No one knowingly enters partnerships with the intention to fail, but too many people fail to do easy and obvious homework, and ask the necessary, direct questions before jumping into a partnership. Remember, "if you don't ask for it, you won't get it", whatever it is, and "it" may be the critical thing you are buying. *Caveat emptor!* (Translation: *"let the buyer beware!"*)

> So much is written about wonderful partnerships that seem to work so well that we forget that many partnerships fail, some doomed from the outset. If more were written about the ones that don't work and why, we might learn more about the questions to ask and information to seek before entering a partnership or alliance. Do your homework – "forewarned is forearmed." Don't assume anything – ask! Always restate the good reasons for forming the partnership to keep them in the forefront of everyone's thinking, but don't be naive!

NOTES

1 Rosen, Robert (2000) *Global Literacies*. Simon & Schuster, New York.
2 Rosen, ibid.
3 Graham, Mark (2001) *IndustryWeek*, March 5.

Key Concepts and Thinkers

This chapter draws out key concepts in the field of partnerships that help in clarifying and defining the field. A number of recent developments based on partnering are introduced and described, and a useful assessment tool is included.

FORMS OF BUSINESSES

There are five common forms of business ownership in the United States and comparable forms in other countries. Laws and business forms vary widely, so check your country's laws before making decisions on partnerships. www.IFCWorld.com provides a number of more extensive descriptions of business ownership forms, including many that span different countries.

- Partnership
- Sole proprietorship
- Corporation
- Limited liability company
- Limited partnership.

A partnership is defined as a business owned by two or more people. Each partner can perform all of the actions required to operate the business: making decisions, hiring people, spending money, borrowing money, etc. Each partner is personally liable for *all* of the debts incurred by the partnership – and that includes those that another partner incurs! If your partnership has a claim against it and its assets are not sufficient to fulfill that claim, your personal assets can be taken to pay for business debts. Before you ask – yes, your partner can make agreements and create obligations that you are liable for!

This is why most of the partnerships I am talking about in this book are between people who are part of business entities that have considered these liability issues and taken care of them – that is, by forming corporations, LLCs, etc.

> "Of all of the dozens of business strategies available today, none offers both the potentially rich rewards and the devastating risks of partnership."
>
> *Stephen M. Dent*[1]

LEGAL PARTNERSHIPS (UNITED STATES)

In legal partnerships, partners share in profits or losses in whatever proportion they have agreed to. Any profit or loss is reported on his/her own personal income tax return. Although there is no legal filing requirement for partnership agreements, you can see why they are highly advisable. A great reference for forming legal partnerships is *The Partnership Book*,[2] which describes the steps (and pitfalls) for forming legal partnerships.

There are some things *partners cannot* legally do. Here are a few examples.

» A partner cannot secretly obtain for himself/herself an opportunity available to the partnership.
» Partnership assets cannot be diverted for personal use.
» Partners cannot fail to distribute partnership profits to other members.

There are certainly more of these, but this just gives you an idea of some common partnership "don'ts."

"Limited partnerships" are a different animal, and there are legal requirements for them. These have a "General partner" who really runs things, and "Limited partners" who are basically investors. That means they fall under security laws. LLCs have many of the benefits of partnerships and provide protection from the liability being passed on to put personal assets at risk – thus the name "*Limited liability* company."

Get professional advice

The smart thing to do is to engage the services of qualified professionals – attorneys and/or accountants – familiar with the laws and regulations of the country (countries) where your partnership(s) will be operating, to help you structure any legal partnerships, especially those that might incur liabilities. Otherwise, you may (unknowingly) put your personal wealth/possessions at risk, and that is *not* a smart thing to do!

The Uniform Partnership Act was adopted widely in the United States (in most, but not all states – check with your state) to define some of these rules of partnerships, and provide awareness and warnings to those entering legal partnerships. If your country has such a law, its provisions will likely cover any partnership you form – so check it out, and make sure you comply.

Oral agreements = misunderstandings

Oral partnership agreements are usually not advisable. It is too easy to have misunderstandings which are simply impossible to resolve.

Memories are inaccurate, and become more so under pressure. Even minor disagreements can escalate into major arguments. Partners do not have to be "equal partners" in partnerships – in fact many times they are not. In professional partnerships (lawyers, doctors, etc.) all partners must be members of the profession. Partners in legal partnerships usually don't get salaries; they periodically take an agreed-upon share of the income from the business (this is often called a "draw").

Not every activity of joining interests makes people partners, either for tax purposes or legally. Mere co-owners might not be partners provided that they don't actively carry on a business with whatever they own jointly. Sharing of expenses for a project doesn't necessarily make people "legal" partners either – but it might, so do your homework! Finally, remember this point again: partners, as well as the partnership, are liable for the legal obligations of the partnership – personally!

Communicate

If you and your prospective partner have agreed on the goals and objectives, measures and feedback, then you must also agree on when, where, and how communications will occur to keep the relationship working smoothly and minimizing unnecessary friction. Some friction – not too much – is fine, normal, and even healthy. Too much heats things up and when things get heated up (like tempers) bad results usually follow.

> "Partnership comes in various forms: alliances, mergers, content-sharing deals. Call it what you will, everyone is doing it ... [According to] a recent Forrester Research study, 84 percent said the aspect of their business most likely to grow in the next year would be partnerships, far outpacing staffing, technology, content, and product offerings.
> *James Daly, editor in chief, BUSINESS 2.0*

ALLIANCES VS. PARTNERSHIPS – "THE SAME, BUT DIFFERENT THAN PARTNERSHIPS"

Many people use the terms partnership and alliance interchangeably, and while that may be generally OK, there is a difference in what the two terms mean. Partnership is a deeper, more committed relationship than

KEY CONCEPTS AND THINKERS

an alliance, although an alliance can develop into a partnership – more often than vice versa. Many experts have commented on these semantic issues, so I will use their words to explain further.

> "Conventional partnerships serve set objectives and face well-circumscribed risks; their economics are usually clearly understood from the start, and their strategic scope is usually limited and clearly bounded ... Not so in the strategic alliance, in which the partners must be flexible and must see theirs as a relationship whose objectives are bound to evolve in ways that cannot be fully planned at the inception."[3]

> "I use the term alliance to mean cooperation between groups that produces better results than can be gained from a transaction ... There is a night and day difference between transactions and alliances. In transactions, contracts spell out everything ... In an alliance, you can't define every detail. Success depends on creatively joining the ideas and energies of the two firms."[4]

> "In a partnership, the interests are undivided. In an alliance, there is a pact or agreement between the parties to cooperate for a specific purpose and to merge their separate interests and efforts for that common purpose. The pact ... establishing their alliance ... provides for flexibility. It also recognizes that their interests will differ at times."[5]

Finally I'll turn to a leading consulting firm's definition, because it is perhaps the most complete:

"DEFINING THE BEAST: WHAT IS AN ALLIANCE?"[6]

We define a strategic alliance as a cooperative arrangement between two or more companies where:

» A common strategy is developed in unison and a win-win attitude is adopted by all parties.
» The relationship is reciprocal, with each partner prepared to share specific strengths with each other, thus lending power to the enterprise.

> » A pooling of resources, investment, and risks occurs for mutual (rather than individual) gain.

"In a strategic alliance firms cooperate out of mutual need and share the risks to reach a common objective ... If they don't share significant risks they can't expect mutual commitments. Firms will share risks only if they need each other to reach the same objective."

Jordan D. Lewis[7]

ASSESSMENT OF PARTNERSHIP SUCCESS

To determine the probability of success of prospective partnerships or to assess the health of current partnerships, the Assessment of Partnership Success below is a useful tool. Both partners should complete it independently and then discuss the results openly. This will reveal probable trouble spots and also expose differences in perception and opinion that could lead to further difficulties.

Rate each topic from 1 = very poor, 2 = somewhat poor, 3 = average, 4 = somewhat good, 5 = very good.

ITEM		SCORE
1	Choice of partners *(Is this a strategically valuable partner for your business?)*	...
2	Willingness to become a partner *(Does this partner desire to become your partner?)*	...
3	Trust *(Is there a good level of trust or the possibility of one?)*	...
4	Character and ethics *(Has experience proven this exists or can exist?)*	...

5	Strategic intent *(Do the aspirations of both partners match or are they compatible?)*	...
6	Culture fit *(Do the partners have similar or compatible cultures?)*	...
7	Consistent directions *(Is there a consistent direction for partnering efforts – on both parties' behalf?)*	...
8	Common goals and interests *(Are the goals and interests of the partners shared fairly equally?)*	...
9	Information sharing *(Can both partners feel good about liberal information sharing?)*	...
10	Risks shared fairly *(Are the risks to both partners fairly equal?)*	...
11	Rewards shared fairly *(Are the rewards and potential gains for both partners fairly equal?)*	...
12	Resources adequately matched *(Does the smaller partner have adequate resources to support the larger?)*	...
13	Duration mutually agreed long term *(Do the partners agree on a long-term partnership?)*	...
14	Sponsors in top management of both *Is there good top management support at both partners?)*	...
15	Commitment to partnership by both *Is there a fairly broad level of commitment by both partners?)*	...
16	Value given and received *Do both partners have "grossly similar" perceptions of the value of the other?)*	...

| 17 | Rules, policies, and measures *Do these key measures reinforce the desired partnership behavior?)* **TOTAL SCORE** | ... ... |

CPFR (COLLABORATIVE PLANNING, FORECASTING, AND REPLENISHMENT)

One of the hottest new partnership tools is an approach called CPFR. What is it? CPFR is a cross-industry initiative designed to improve supplier–customer relationships through co-managing the planning and sharing of responsibility for the forecasting and replenishment of goods – primarily for retailers.

This process, developed by a US group called the Voluntary Interindustry Commerce Standards (VICS) Association, defines the best practices and protocols to make CPFR work for the partners who use it. This initiative began a few years ago with consultancy Benchmark Partners (now named Surgency), large suppliers like Warner-Lambert, and large customers like Wal-Mart seeking a better way to stay in stock, reduce inventory, and improve communications. Supply chain software companies like i2 and Manugistics and several ERP software firms (ASI/Logility, to name one) were also involved early in the CPFR process. Many more are involved now.

A pilot project involved Warner-Lambert's Listerine® mouthwash sold via Wal-Mart stores. The process was first used in a paper-based form and then demonstrated on a computer. In-stock positions for Listerine rose from 87% to 98%, lead times dropped from 21 to 11 days, and sales increased by $8.5 million over the test period even though the test was limited to one Warner-Lambert plant and only three Wal-Mart distribution centers. This was clearly a powerful partnership tool.

"In this era of corporate partnering people have to work together not only across oceans but sometimes across deeper divides of corporate boundaries and corporate cultures"
Jon Katzenbach and Douglas Smith (2001) FORBES.COM, May 21

The purpose of CPFR is to reduce or eliminate uncertainty through improved communications between supply chain trading partners. The key word in the name is "collaborative."

Collaborate is defined by *Merriam Webster's Collegiate Dictionary* as: 1. To work together, especially in a joint effort, and 2. To cooperate treasonably as with an enemy occupation force in one's country.

What a strange way to describe collaboration – "to cooperate treasonably." This is not as surprising as it might seem, because true collaboration (as in the first definition) is rare enough within companies, and rarer still between companies!

The keys to making CPFR work require changes in behavior of the people at the partners – a real challenge. The difficulty is getting all of those using the process to consistently act in the spirit of the collaborative process. Trust is the issue in most collaborative partnerships and this one is no exception. If both partners in the CPFR process realize that the end consumer is their customer, and behave accordingly, the process can work wonders. When they don't, it makes only minor improvements.

Wal-Mart's RetailLink system allows its suppliers to have unparalleled visibility of the performance and status of the goods in its stores and distribution system. This kind of open information sharing is a hallmark of partnership. Although both companies don't overtly call it CPFR, the Manco-Wal-Mart relationship is one of the more productive ones using this methodology. Why? Because the people act, feel, and work like partners. That is the only way any of these new initiatives will realize the greatest benefits for the partners involved.

CRM/PRM (CUSTOMER RELATIONSHIP MANAGEMENT/PARTNER RELATIONSHIP MANAGEMENT)

CRM is a popular acronym ("buzzword") for age-old processes translated to the new computer/Web-based economy. Its devotees describe it as "the overall process of marketing, sales, and service within any organization." Others describe it differently: "a business strategy to get, grow, and retain the right customers, leading to long-term profitability." As customer service expectations continue to escalate, more companies, especially larger ones, are turning to CRM to help integrate their far-flung dealings with customers.

PRM (Partner Relationship Management) is a subset of CRM, and is "the application of relationship management strategies and technologies to the unique needs of indirect sales channels." CRM and PRM systems are supposed to help businesses develop and sustain profitable customer/channel partner relationships – and maybe they do. At least the software industry is hoping to sell about $2 billion of supporting systems in the next two–three years. The good news is the attention being paid to serving customer partners more effectively.

> "Customer Relationship Management (CRM) is a business strategy to select and manage customer relationships to optimize long-term value to an enterprise. CRM requires a customer-centric business philosophy and culture to support effective marketing, sales and service processes across all direct and indirect customer interaction channels. CRM software applications can enable effective Customer Relationship Management, provided an enterprise has the right strategy, leadership, and culture."
>
> *www.CRMGuru.com*

Companies are investing in CRM in hopes of becoming more effective in their selling while gaining competitive differentiation in a world where pricing is globally transparent and products become commodities overnight. But there is no replacement for good old-fashioned customer relationships – between people! What CRM will do is provide a multi-channel tool for people to share what is happening and how customer needs and company capabilities can be best matched – and that is a very good thing to do.

Key functional areas of CRM include:

» Marketing automation – Targets the best customers, manages marketing campaigns, generates quality leads, and shares the information easily.
» Sales automation – Supports the selling process from lead qualification to closing the business.
» Customer service – Resolves customer issues responsively after the sale, building customer satisfaction and loyalty.

» E-commerce – Handles the transaction online, as a seamless extension of the sales process.

Information should flow easily between these functional areas, facilitating collaborative team selling and support. This can be accomplished with CRM suites or by integrating best-of-breed solutions. Increasingly, Internet-based CRM and PRM systems are the norm, providing a common platform to deliver applications for use by employees, partners, and customers.

"As a rule, however, enterprises have re-discovered the importance of channel partners"[8]

Tips for winning with CRM[9]

- » **Deliver value first**. Your customers don't care about your management problems. Make sure their experience is one that will motivate them to return again and again, and to make positive referrals.
- » **It's still about people**. Technology is great, but without executive leadership, employee and partner buy-in, and a genuine emotional bond with your customers, a CRM project won't be successful.
- » **Pick CRM partners, not vendors**. Find software and service firms that are as committed to you as you are to your customers. In other words, pick CRM technology partners that practice good CRM.
- » **"Ready, aim, fire" doesn't work**. Resist the temptation to make it up as you go. CRM is complex. Use process analysis and planning methodologies to avoid costly and time-consuming rework later on. Installing software means nothing.
- » **Treat partners like customers**. You can't do it all alone; get some help! To win the battle for mind share with indirect sales channels, invest in tools to enable partners to do business more effectively and efficiently.

"The future prosperity of a business depends on its ability to initiate, sustain, and profit from interdependent relationships. Successful businesses develop relationships. Relationships can become creative partnerships and reflect the values of people working with trust and respect for each other."

Stephen M. Dent[10]

DRM[11] (DYNAMIC RESOURCE MANAGEMENT)

A trio of technologies is coming together, which can pay off big for business when used correctly. PCs, the Internet, and searchable databases combined in new applications will make instant sense of information, and let companies analyze data on the spot in order to respond to constantly changing conditions and rapidly – "turn on a dime."

A common name for these new tools has been coined – dynamic resource management (DRM); also known as "control towers," and "executive dashboards," such tools have tremendous potential to cut costs, serve customers better, boost profits, and create competitive advantages.

The catalyst for all this is a convergence of multiple rapidly evolving technologies:

- » Cheaper, faster, more portable PCs that can rapidly analyze complicated "what if?" scenarios anywhere, anytime.
- » XML (Extensible Markup Language) software that puts data in a universally understood format.
- » Broadband pipelines that can move huge volumes of information over the Internet and around the world, faster than ever.
- » Clear wireless transmission bringing data to the factory floor, the retail floor, the delivery truck, or the remote job site . . . and more.
- » Smarter software that can spot and fix errors and make basic, routine decisions.
- » Software applications that integrate the plethora of old and new systems in use, and that can convert current programs into a single language, letting machinery and systems communicate and interact.

This concept can mean finely tuned management of resources and suppliers, from electricity to paper, capital needs to telecommunications services, as well as systems with end-to-end supply chain visibility that can enable rapid yet insightful juggling of suppliers and materials and meet exact production and customer needs faster than ever and at lower costs than ever.

This daily choreographing of production lines to match demand changes will help avoid costly inventory bloat and immediately capitalize on consumer trends. Production bottlenecks will become less and less frequent, and most can be identified *before* they develop, and alleviated. All of this will allow groups of partners to make "overnight" shifts in sales strategies as opportunities are spotted, and then capitalize on those opportunities to the advantage of all partners. It is an emerging embodiment of the value network described earlier – right before our eyes.

Of course, there is a *huge* caveat to all this: partners must be closely linked and prepared to use this technology collaboratively – or it will all be wasted. Only a minor part of today's technology is utilized with high levels of effectiveness, not because companies do not have it, and not because they don't know how to use it. The lack of success anywhere near the potential of the technology is a people issue – more appropriately a lack of trust issue among the people who must make the technology really "hum."

A handful of large companies already use custom-made DRM systems, but most are targeted at controlling specific aspects of internal production and supplies. The earlier example describes how Dell Computer captures orders and triggers production needs on the spot. Apparel maker Esprit's system is helping the company double its sales volume, slash inventories by tracking sales in real time, and then revamping orders with global sources. Zara controls its own factories and stores and links them with rapid response, near real-time information. Procter & Gamble, Warner-Lambert, Manco, Wal-Mart, and other leading companies are also reaping the benefits of this information-enabled collaboration.

A few of the most notable "leading-edge DRM systems" in use now are:

» Silicon Energy's utilities monitor;
» Sun Microsystems' network governor;
» transportation supply chain manager from Logistics.com (another from Capstan); and
» "plant in a laptop" from Executive Manufacturing Technology to control/monitor production.

The benefits can be substantial – some companies estimate cuts of 20% in utility bills, materials waste down 30%, full payback in three months! But custom systems cost big bucks, running to a million dollars or more for most big jobs. There are smaller systems, with rock-bottom prices only for narrower tasks, at pricing more like $50,000. But prices will continue to fall as more developers jump on the bandwagon and into the market with affordable systems designed for small businesses.

In the next year of two, DRM systems will be widespread in big business, a key tool for managing specific, capital-intensive, critical sectors like energy, telecommunications, and logistics. In less than five years, systems aimed at smaller businesses and encompassing nearly all company operations will be commonplace.

The impact on business will be broad and deep, another leap forward in productivity. But the conditions of partnerships must be met for this new technology to realize anywhere near its full potential. There will be even less impetus for vertical integration but the need for much closer ties between suppliers, makers, and sellers will grow.

The role of middle management will change again, as more decisions are made directly by top execs or frontline supervisors with the help of these systems. The job of middle management will become that of partnership builder, systems integrator, and critical liaison – and no longer that of message carrier or politician.

MEASUREMENTS

The old saying "what gets measured, gets done" is all too true. My old friend and author Will Kaydos puts it another way: "If you can't measure it, you can't manage it." This means that all successful partnerships require measurements, and the measurements must be meaningful and supportive of the intent of the partnership.

Since the supply chain is a good partnership model, the concept of measurement in the supply chain is a good place to start. Peter Brewer and Tom Speh comment on this exact topic when they say:[12]

"First ... companies ... must work collaboratively. A true supply chain is defined by inter-company collaboration – and the supply chain performance measurement system should reflect this. Second, in the supply chain environment, both companies and individual managers must be motivated to work in collaboration with supply chain partners. Because performance measurement systems influence behavior ('you get what you measure'), the performance measurement process must be structured to provide incentives for collaborative behavior."

Work out the measures as you work out the partnership. Unless both partners have deep-seated equity in the measures, there will not be the kind of "buy-in" that is so essential to success. Make the measures quantitative, clear, and relatively few; then communicate them widely so all affected parties know what they are and how things are going!

"Core competencies are quite simply what an organization is best-in-world at. Everything else is somebody else's core competency and is better acquired through a strategic relationship with that firm ... No company alone can possibly hope to out-innovate all the competitors, potential competitors, suppliers, and external knowledge sources in its marketplace worldwide."

James Brian Quinn

STRATEGIC OUTSOURCING

So often, terms like strategic outsourcing are abused. These terms are used to describe arrangements that are not strategic at all, but rather are opportunistic or convenient. Strategic outsourcing is the term that goes back to the primary premise of why to partner – no company can be good enough at everything!

Research done for The Outsourcing Research Council by Michael F. Corbitt & Associates showed that 3000 US companies with more than a half-billion dollars each in revenue will spend 7% of that revenue – that's $875 billion in total, heading toward a trillion dollars – on outsourcing. Outsourcing is clearly big business. Not only that, but almost every industry in the study projected outsourcing to grow at a 15–25% rate *per year* for the foreseeable future. That's a lot of working together. No wonder making partnerships work is an important topic.

Outsourcing permits companies to focus valuable resources on their core competencies and not dilute them trying to be ATTAP (All Things To All People). For outsourcing to be truly strategic, it is important to consider the reasons for the outsourcing and what is to be gained by it.

» Why (strategy) – to beat the competition, make more money, do it faster, better, and always to serve the customer better.

- » Where (execution) – where you can't do it alone (which is almost always), so you can concentrate on what you are best at doing.
- » Who (selection) – choosing the partner to trust for the things you're not good at.
- » What (need) – you cannot afford to be good enough at everything, so choosing what to be good at is a critical decision.
- » When (timing) – as soon as you realize you should – like right now!

If you truly understand the reasons for using partnerships and outsourcing – how and when to use alliances, partnerships, different forms of working together – then you will be on the road to doing *strategic* outsourcing. If you learn why, where, and when to use partnerships as part of strategic outsourcing and understand why strong, effective outsourcing depends on partnering, then you will be on the road to making partnerships really work for you and your company.

NOTES

1 Dent, Stephen M. (1999) *Partnering Intelligence*. Davies-Black, Palo Alto, CA.
2 *The Partnership Book*, www.nolo.com.
3 Doz, Yves & Hamel, Gary (1998) *Alliance Advantage*. Harvard Business School Press, Boston, MA.
4 Lewis, Jordan D. (1990) *Partnerships for Profit*. The Free Press, New York.
5 Lynch, Clifford F. (2000) "Managing the outsourcing relationship." *Supply Chain Management Review*, September–October.
6 Booz-Allen & Hamilton (1993) "A Practical Guide to Alliances: Leapfrogging the Learning Curve." New York.
7 Lewis, ibid.
8 "CRM and the Internet – leading edge strategies for a multi-channel world." *Business Week*, April 30, (2001).
9 Ibid.

10 Dent, ibid.
11 Derived from the Kiplinger Forecasting Newsletter, May (2001).
12 Brewer, Peter C. & Speh, Thomas W. (2001) "Adapting the balanced scorecard to supply chain management." *Supply Chain Management Review*, March–April.

Resources

This chapter provides an excellent overview of books and Websites that the reader can use to build a broader understanding of the field of partnerships and alliances.

INTRODUCTION

Contemporary business publications are full of partnership stories. It is almost impossible to go through one without finding several. A few of the most useful are listed below with the titles and sources. In most cases these publications archive the articles on their Websites. Many times, an article, particularly those that grow into books (often done by publications like the *Harvard Business Review* and Harvard Business School Press), provide most of the useful information, without the time demands of reading an entire book.

PERIODICALS

FORBES.COM, *Best of The Web* Special Issue: Strategic Alliance Guide, May 21, 2001.

"Competing for supply." <u>Conversation</u>, *Harvard Business Review*, February, 2001.

"Hardball is still GM's game." *Business Week*, August 8, 1994, 26. www.businessweek.com

"McDonald's conquers the world." *Fortune*, October 17, 1994, 103-16. www.fortune.com

"Supply chain collaboration - close encounters of the best kind." *Business Week*, March 26, 2001. www.businessweek.com

Das, T.K. & Teng, Bing-Sheng (1998) "Between trust and control: developing confidence in partner cooperation in alliances." *Academy of Management Review*, Baruch College, CUNY.

Drucker, Peter F. (1995) "The network society." *The Wall Street Journal*, March 29. www.wsj.com

Enslow, Beth, (2000) VP, Descartes Systems Group, from "The glass pipeline." *Supply Chain Management Software Supplement*, Cahners. www.scmr.com

Graham, Mark (2000) *IndustryWeek*, March 5. www.industryweek.com

Hamel, Gary (2000) "Reinventing competition." *Executive Excellence*, January. www.eep.com

Hansen, Morten, Chesbrough, Henry, Nohria, Nitin, & Sull, Donald (2000) "Networked incubators - hothouses of the new economy." *Harvard Business Review*, September–October. www.hbsp.harvard.com

Jap, Sandy (2000) "Going, going, gone." *Harvard Business Review*, November-December.

Kahl, Jack (1993) "The ethics of partnership." *Duck Tales*, November-December. www.manco.com

Kelly, Jim (2000) "Managing the speed of business." *Executive Excellence*, January. www.eepcom

LaLonde, Bud (2000) *Supply Chain Management Review*, September-October. www.scmr.com

Lynch, Clifford F. (2000) "Managing the outsourcing relationship." *Supply Chain Management Review*, September-October. www.scmr.com

Maltz, Arnold (1997) "Switch partners or keep dancing?" *Transportation and Distribution*, July.

McLean, Bethany (1999) "Merging at INTERNET SPEED." *Fortune*, November 8. www.fortune.com

Mentzer, John T., Foggin, James H., & Golicic, Susan L. (2000) "Collaboration - the enablers, impediments, and benefits." *Supply Chain Management Review*, September-October. www.scmr.com

Prahalad, C.K. & Hamel, Gary (1990) "The core competence of the corporation." *Harvard Business Review*, May-June, 79-91. www.hbsp.harvard.com

Shelton, Ken (1993) "Partners: worth their weight in gold." *Executive Excellence*, 10 (No. 11), 2. www.eep.com

Stalk, George, Jr. (1988) "Time - the next source of competitive advantage." *Harvard Business Review*, July-August, 41-51. www.hbsp.harvard.com

Stalk, George, Evans, Philip, & Shulman, Lawrence E. (1992) "Competing on capabilities: the new rules of corporate strategy." *Harvard Business Review*, March-April, 57-69. www.hbsp.harvard.com

Treacy, Michael & Wiersma, Fred (1993) "Customer intimacy and other value disciplines." *Harvard Business Review*, January-February, 84-93. www.hbsp.harvard.com

Womack, James & Jones, Daniel (1993) "From lean production to the lean enterprise." *Harvard Business Review*, March-April, 93-103. www.hbsp.harvard.com

CONSULTANTS

In many cases leading consulting organizations publish excellent works on topics like partnerships. Surgency, formerly named Benchmarking Partners, has done a lot of work in this field. Just a couple of many others are cited here. Most major consultancies claim to have expertise in this field, but not many have real in-depth expertise – I find that many have superficial competency. The authors of books listed in this section are often consultants who have far more in-depth partnership skills than large, general-purpose consulting companies.

"A Practical Guide to Alliances: Leapfrogging the Learning Curve – a perspective for U.S. companies." *Viewpoint*, Booz-Allen and Hamilton, New York, 1993.

"Partnerships: creating synergy." Training materials for the course Strategies for High-Involvement Leadership. Developmental Dimensions International, Pittsburgh, PA, 1994. www.ddiworld.com

Rogers, Robert, COO, Development Dimensions International, in *The Psychological Contract of Trust*. Pittsburgh, PA, 1994. www.ddiworld.com

BOOKS

Of course there are numerous books on the subject of partnerships and alliances and the strategies underlying the relationships. In addition to my own books, books by noted authors like Jordan Lewis and Gary Hamel as well as many others have addressed this important topic aimed specifically at given aspects of partnering. Here is a short list of what I consider the best ones to read or skim.

Legal focus

Partnerships are legal entities in many cases. Knowing what you can and cannot do, what you are and are not liable for, and how the assets and proceeds of the partnership are divided can be critical issues. Partnership agreements are often necessary. Government reporting may be required. A couple of sources for most if not all of these answers are very useful tools for prospective partners.

The Partnership Book. www.Nolo.com
www.ifcworld.com

Relationship focus

Above all else, partnerships are relationships – sometimes between companies, and always between people. Dent deals with the human side of partnerships very effectively and provides assessments and diagnostic tools that will prove useful. Lewis has been studying and writing about partnerships at least as long as I have, and provides a wonderful breadth of perspective.

Melohn, the Reinas, and McGregor offer human insights that will be useful, especially in partnering with employees. So does Maslow's historic work, now reprinted with notes by Warren Bennis and others.

Sam Walton epitomized the ultimate business success based on partnerships, and his autobiography (the official one – listed – not the other one) is an education in itself, and recommended reading for everyone.

Dent, Stephen M. (1999) *Partnering Intelligence*. Davies-Black, Palo Alto, CA.
Lewis, Jordan (1999) *Trusted Partners*. The Free Press, New York.
Mariotti, John L. (1996) *The Power of Partnerships*. Blackwell, Oxford.
Maslow, Abraham (1998) *Maslow on Management*. Wiley, New York.
McGregor, Douglas (1985) *The Human Side of Enterprise*. McGraw-Hill, New York.
Melohn, Tom, (1994) *The New Partnership*. Omneo, an imprint of Oliver Wight Publications, Essex Junction, NH.
Reina, Dennis & Reina, Michelle (1999) *Trust and Betrayal in the Workplace*. Berrett-Koehler, San Francisco, CA.
Walton, Sam, with John Huey (1992) *Made in America, My Story*. Doubleday Books, New York.

Strategy focus

The issue of why, when, and how to do partnerships and alliances is often a critical strategic decision. Thus I have listed one of the most insightful strategists of this decade, Gary Hamel, as a primary resource. Hamel's articles in the *Harvard Business Review* with C.K. Prahalad dating back to 1989 are also worthy reading. Jordan Lewis's works have dealt with the strategic implications of partnering and contain many useful examples. Of course no reading list in this era would be complete without the "grand poohbah" of management books, my old friend Tom Peters.

Tom throws so many mental hand grenades that your mind is bound to be disturbed – and that is what he wants. He wants you to get out of your comfort zone and think! Womack *et al.* contributed a valuable addition to management thought in their analysis of the vaunted Toyota Production System and the concept of "Lean Production" – a concept which is as valid today as it was a couple of decades ago when the name was invented.

Doz, Yves & Hamel, Gary (1998) *Alliance Advantage*. Harvard Business School Press, Boston, MA.

Hamel, Gary (2000) *Leading the Revolution*. Harvard Business School Press, Boston, MA.

Lewis, Jordan (1990) *Partnerships for Profit: Structuring and Managing Strategic Alliances*. The Free Press, New York.

Lewis, Jordan (1995) *The Connected Corporation*. The Free Press, New York.

Mariotti, John L. (1997) *The Shape Shifters – Continuous Change for Competitive Advantage*. Wiley, New York.

Peters, Thomas J. (1992) *Liberation Management*. Alfred A. Knopf, New York.

Peters, Thomas J. & Waterman, Robert H. (1982) *In Search of Excellence*. Harper and Row, New York.

Sujansky, Joanne G. (1991) *Power of Partnering: Vision, Commitment, and Action*. Pfeiffer, San Diego, CA.

Womack, James P., Jones, Daniel T., & Roos, Daniel (1990) *The Machine That Changed the World*. Rawson, a division of Macmillan, New York.

Global focus

The greatest management thinker of the twentieth century is now in his nineties and his mind is as sharp and insightful as ever. You can read any or all of Peter Drucker's books and come away richer and wiser. His latest is the only one I have listed, but they are all, in varying degrees, wonderful.

Tom Friedman's book is an essential read for global thinking. It is not a management book *per se*; it is rather an observation of the global scene with conclusions as to what is working how and why. Charles Handy has been rocking the foundations of conventional thought from his garden in England for the past 10 years, and any of his books will be useful. They are all entertaining and insightful, as is Robert Rosen's book on twenty-first-century global leadership and culture.

Drucker, Peter F. (1999) *Management Challenges for the 21st Century*. Harper, New York.
Friedman, Thomas (1999, 2000) *The Lexus and the Olive Tree*. Anchor Books, New York.
Handy, Charles (1994) *The Age of Paradox*. Random House, London.
Rosen, Robert (2000) *Global Literacies*. Simon & Schuster, New York.

Change focus

Above all else, partnering requires change. There are many books about change. Simple little books like Spencer Johnson's bestseller will open your mind. Books like the one by Rick Maurer will help you in recognizing resistance to change and understanding what to do about it.

Johnson, Spencer (1998) *Who Moved my Cheese?* Putnam, New York.
Maurer, Rick (1996) *Beyond the Wall of Resistance*. Bard, Dallas, TX.

Ten Steps to Making it Work

This chapter describes a progression of steps that must be taken for organizations to build and sustain successful partnerships. A "how to get started" list is provided.

Always remember these 10 partnership steps.

An important reminder: Most partnerships that succeed follow a progression approximately like these 10 steps, and although the order may vary, all of these steps will be covered. Most partnerships that fail are doomed almost from the very start/early stages because they fail to face known issues and problems early and resolve them at the outset, when it is far easier than after investments of time, money, and ego are made by both partners.

1. CHOICE: CHOOSE CAREFULLY AND WISELY – IS THIS AN IMPORTANT AND VALUABLE PARTNER?

The first, most critical, and frequently overlooked success factor in forming partnerships is the choice of a partner. There are many criteria for choosing a partner, but need and "fit" are good ones. Do both of the partners need something that the other can provide? Do the two partners seem to naturally fit with each other?

How has this prospective partner's track record been at forming partnerships? A bad track record – one with a litany of excuses for failed partnerships – is a strong warning against joining the list of former, failed partners.

On the other hand, a good track record is a great endorsement. If the prospective partner encourages you to talk to other partners, by all means do so. Take the time to do your homework and don't rush headlong into a partnership that will consume time, energy, and resources, only to fail anyway.

2. WILLINGNESS: ARE YOU WILLING TO BE A PARTNER, AND IS YOUR PARTNER?

It is really hard, perhaps impossible, to form a partnership with an unwilling or even very reluctant partner. Such a statement seems so obvious, yet so many companies become so enchanted with their own plans and wishes that they fail to notice the reticence on the part of the prospective partner.

A good idea is to ask – "Are you willing to partner with us on this?" Then listen closely to the answer. If this prospect is a large supplier to you, it may not want to say "no" in so many words, but its answer will give you the clues you need. Although the Japanese have no specific words for "no," their statements like "it is most difficult" tell all you need to know.

If the answers contain reservations and concerns with little or no enthusiasm for the potential of the partnership, you have your answer. Trying to change the mind of an unwilling partner is a low-percentage way to spend your time. The only time worth doing this is when this partner is the "only viable option" to achieve what you desire - but even then, unwilling partners don't form strong partnerships. They are always looking for the things that go wrong instead of the things that go right.

3. TRUST: DOES TRUST ALREADY EXIST OR CAN IT BE BUILT (OR REBUILT)?

No trust means no true partnership. Period. Trust is like a balloon. You strain and struggle to blow it up, and you let it go for just a second and the air rushes out if it. And yet, without trust, there can be no meaningful partnership.

Trust is a two-way street. To gain trust, you must be trustworthy, and vice versa for your partner. Trust is about sharing openly. Trust cannot happen overnight, even if one or both partners want it to. To build trust requires time and experience with each other. There must be deposits made in the "bank account" of trust. Small withdrawals may occur, and these must be openly acknowledged and discussed as soon as they occur. Trust can be built only by dealing with concerns and issues, and resolving conflicts before they can fester and become serious.

Finally, if you can trust your partner, you don't have to ask about it. You know it. Behaviors speak far louder than words. When issues come up that are uncertain or look like they might harm the trusting relationship, partners discuss them openly - even argue about them - but then they resolve them. Trust is balanced on a tightrope, midway between faith and doubt, and it cannot ever move too far toward doubt, or it falls off the tightrope. Some actions build trust; others "bust" trust. Look at the list below so you know which ones to favor and which to avoid.

TRUST BUILDERS AND TRUST BUSTERS[1]

Top 10 trust builders

- » Discuss
- » Recognize
- » Support
- » Collaborate
- » Disclose
- » Value
- » Help
- » Acknowledge
- » Share
- » Ask.

Top 10 trust busters

- » Hide
- » Blame
- » Defend
- » Argue
- » Mislead
- » Ignore
- » Intimidate
- » Abdicate
- » Punish
- » Assume.

4. "CHIPS" (CHARACTER, HONESTY, INTEGRITY, AND PRINCIPLES) MUST BE THERE – ARE THEY?

This is a memorable little acronym I coined to help remember some of the critical characteristics that must exist for trust to be built and thus for partnerships to succeed.

> char· ac· ter (kàr'ek-ter) noun. The combination of qualities or features that distinguishes one person, group, or thing from another.[2]

Character is a part of what a person is, does, and believes in. Character is often evident, but adept charlatans can conceal the lack of it until the "chips are down" and then it shows – or doesn't. A person of character stands up for what they believe in, even when it isn't popular. This is one of the most common clues. A person of good character says what they'll do and then does what they said. And this leads to the next one of the CHIPs – honesty.

> hon· es· ty (òn'ĭstê) noun. The quality or condition of being honest; integrity. Truthfulness; sincerity[3]

Honesty is all about doing what you said, after saying what you'd do. It is about truthfulness too. Honesty is next door to fairness. An honest person doesn't try to take unfair advantage of another. Honesty doesn't mean saying harmful things that don't have to be said, but it does mean raising sticky issues when they exist – before they cause problems.

> in· teg· ri· ty (ĭn-tèg'rĭtê) noun. Steadfast adherence to a strict moral or ethical code.[4]

Integrity starts to cover some of the same ground as honesty and character. Integrity is like virginity: you either have it or you don't – there is no part way. A secondary definition of integrity describes it as the condition of being whole, or of completeness. That is a good way to think about it too.

> prin· ci· ple (prĭn'se-pel) noun. A basic truth, law, or assumption: the principles of democracy. **a.** A rule or standard, especially of good behavior: a man of principle. **b.** The collectivity of moral or ethical standards or judgments: a decision based on principle rather than expediency.[5]

Author Stephen Covey refers to principles as a "compass" showing true north. There is no negotiability about matters of principle. Just as the case with character, a person with principles doesn't talk about them – he/she believes them. Principles also reinforce the CHIP of honesty. They are rooted in integrity.

Find these CHIPs in a company and its people – especially its top management leadership – and you have likely found a good partner. If they are missing, get out of there. Without CHIPs there can be no trust, and without trust, there can be no partnership. There may be some form of alliance or transaction possible, but be careful.

5. FIT: STRATEGICALLY, STRUCTURALLY, AND CULTURALLY – CAN YOU BOTH MAKE IT WORK?

What does this vague term "fit" mean? It means the same thing as when you try on a pair of shoes – you know if they fit, because they feel good and don't hurt you. Fit in partnerships is a bit more complex. Fit means that you have similar values, and similar aspirations, goals, and objectives. Fit means that you will choose similar paths to reach those aspirations, goals, and objectives.

Two partners who differ greatly in size must realize that their aspirations will differ based on that size difference. Partners that come from different cultures will have to recognize that and both must adjust to help the fit occur without either partner abandoning their culture.

Discussing this topic of "fit" openly can help in both assessing it and aligning it. Often, it is easier to tell when there is not a fit than when there *might* be one. Misfits usually show up in a number of ways, most of which are painful or challenging. If there is a steady stream of conflicts or apparent obstacles, this may signal a poor fit! Don't ignore these warning signs. Make sure there is a good "fit." If there isn't, drop back to an arm's-length transaction and forget about partnering.

6. COMMUNICATION: AND INFORMATION SHARING – WILL YOU AND WILL THEY?

If trust is the critical need for a partnership, then open communications and information sharing are the most visible indicators of the level of trust. It is very difficult to form a strong partnership without open communications, and liberal information sharing. If you don't trust the prospective partner, then you won't want to share information with them, and vice versa.

When a partnership starts to build based on trust, then the partners can take advantage of the power of technology to share information that permits both partners to perform better. The more openly partners communicate and share information, the more effectively they can get to the bottom of issues and head off potential conflicts.

7. GOALS: ARE THEY SHARED, UNDERSTOOD, AND IN A CONSISTENT DIRECTION?

Partnerships are not just "feelgood" exercises. They are intended to help both partners achieve their goals. This assumes that the partners have clearly defined goals and that they know and understand each other's goals. Having a shared understanding of goals makes achieving them much more likely.

If the goals are vague and not specific, then there is a chance that the goals will change mid-stream, causing disconnections in the partners' activities. Writing the goals and sharing them gives them a clarity that is otherwise missing. Just because goals are written doesn't mean they can't change - they will change - but the changes must also be communicated and agreed upon promptly.

Comparing written goals helps assure that there is consistency in the magnitude and direction of the goals. It is surprising how many times this consistency is missing - and the partners don't realize it is causing a problem or conflict. Written goals also help build commitment on the part of all parties (more on that later).

PARTNERSHIP CHECKPOINTS[6]

» Outcomes - What is success, specifics?
» Benefits - What's in it for me/us? (And what do we risk to get how much out of it?)
» Barriers - What problems might we face?
» Approach - How will this partnership work?
» Support - What support do I have or need to provide?
» Measurement - How will we measure results and reward shared success?

8. 3RS (RISKS, REWARDS, AND RESOURCES): ARE THEY FAIRLY BALANCED AND ADEQUATELY UNDERSTOOD?

This topic first came up in the point on "fit." All partnerships have risks and rewards. All partnerships require the commitment of resources. Not all partners have the same tolerance for risk or the same ability to commit resources. Balanced does not mean equal – it means appropriately related. The partner that takes the higher risk has a right to expect a higher reward. The partner that commits the greater resources should expect greater returns. This is only fair.

These issues will arise along the way, but the further along this 10-point list, the more critical they become. Fit deals with some of them, and so does goal setting. Communication is critical to make sure that there is real understanding of the risks, rewards, and resources. Writing the partnership expectations helps clarify them – and that includes specifying the sharing of risks, rewards, and resources. Setting limits on these 3Rs is also a good topic for discussion. Few things ever work out exactly as planned, but what if one of the partner's risk tolerance is exceeded? What if one partner runs out of resources? What if the expected rewards go down? Deal with these issues up front, and they can be resolved properly. Ignore them at your own peril!

9. COMMITMENT: THIS MUST EXIST AT THE TOP, MIDDLE, AND BOTTOM AND ACROSS FUNCTIONS IN BOTH ORGANIZATIONS

Are there "champions" or at least sponsors in both organizations? A "champion" is defined as "an advocate who really cares about the success of a business alliance, a person who knows how to head off train wrecks even when the organizations involved have very different identities and cultures."[7] Commitment must exist top to bottom and across the organization. This level of commitment cannot exist from the very outset. It is built over time. But it must be present in a small group from the beginning or the first serious conflict will derail the partnership.

While sales and purchasing are typical starting places, other parts of the partner organization(s) will be drawn into the partnership.

Cross-functional partnering is very powerful and effective, but makes it harder to achieve commitment. If there is no commitment from top management, the partnership is doomed. Sooner or later some issue (problem/conflict) will arise that requires the strong leadership of senior management. If senior management has not "bought in," it will not support the partnership through successful resolution of this kind of issue. The partnership will then falter and likely fail.

10. MEASURES: DO YOU BOTH KNOW AND AGREE "WHAT IS SUCCESS" AND HOW YOU'LL KNOW IT WHEN YOU ACHIEVE IT?

Partnering without any agreement on what is success is a sure formula for failure. "If you can't measure something, you can't manage it."[8] Create measures – short term, medium term, and long term. Discuss them and make sure those measures are connected to the mutually agreed-upon goals and objectives. Then make sure everyone involved knows "what is success."

Inevitably, some things will go wrong. Conflicts will arise. Unforeseen problems will crop up. Are you both willing to stick together through good times and bad? True partners have to expect some friction and be committed to the value of the partnership enough to work through the problems.

Have you imagined the form this partnership should take? Not all partnerships are the same – in fact, no two are alike. Customize your planned partnership to meet the needs of the partners. There is nothing like a need-driven, mutual dependence to keep partners together. Can you set clear measures that will determine "how you are doing?" I hope so, because that is where the payoff comes. Making partnerships work is hard work – but the payoff can be huge. Make sure you know "what is success" so you'll recognize it when you see it and celebrate together at having achieved it.

Partnering to make the sale

Many times a team must be formed for just a single sales call – but a critical one!

In these cases, the team leader must make sure a series of steps are followed to give the team a chance at success as "partners".

- » Preplan - Meet, even if briefly, before the call - don't just show up!
- » Approach - Agree on the basic approach - the leader must lead this.
- » Review needs - Agree on how to get the prospect talking about their needs.
- » Translate value - What value proposition of your product will lead your presentation?
- » Negotiate - Who will do what, how, and what are the goals and objectives?
- » Build/Partner - Create the relationship that closes the sale - a win-win partnership.
- » Follow - Follow up and follow through - don't drop the ball on the critical delivery.
- » Maintain contact - Build on the start of a single order to a longer-term partnership.

FINALLY: How to get started forming partnerships

Nothing happens until somebody starts doing something - and the same is true for partnerships. After going through pages of information on what to do and not do, examples about what worked and what didn't, and plenty of resources to learn more - are you ready to start?

There is a little story I like - actually it is a riddle.

> Three frogs were sitting on a log. One frog decides to jump off.
> How many frogs are sitting on the log?
> The answer is not 2! The correct answer is still 3!

Why? *Because there is a difference between decision and action.* A decision only leads to results after someone takes action on it! Here is a short action list to get started. As soon as you finish reading it, put down this book and "jump off that log!"

- » Choose the right potential partner as the first, and most critical, step.
- » Then match cultures, goals, aspirations, resources, risks/rewards - in other words, make it a good "fit."
- » Next, define and agree on expectations - this is a must for success.
- » Then sit down and start discussing all of the above.

- » Review it up and down and across your organization and ask your prospective partner to do the same.
- » Get commitment from the organization and enlist buy-in/support from the top.
- » Make sure you know what the specific goals, objectives, and rewards/benefits are to both partner companies. Also make sure you understand the risks and resources required.

Then get started – think *big*, but try small; then adjust and keep going. If it is worth doing, it is worth doing *now*!

- » Use a checklist, not just for choosing partners, but to be sure you observe the dos and don'ts of mismatched cultures, power, and risk/reward imbalances, etc.
- » Develop your own customized assessment checklist, and use it!
- » Look for opportunities for partnering, they won't just jump up and bite you.
- » Expect obstacles and conflict, and plan on working through them.
- » Get support from senior management to help move obstacles. Imagine the potential opportunities if you succeed.
- » And, when partnerships don't work right, use these steps again to see what can be done. Stay positive until you either make it work or decide to take it apart. If it was a mistake, get out of it – spend your time on partnerships that can succeed.
- » Finally, remember that done properly partnerships are tremendously powerful, and that win-win partnerships have the best chance of succeeding and being sustained over a long period of time.

Now you are under way, it is time to go back and check the things you have forgotten that will get in the way of success, and how to deal with them. But at least you are under way! That puts you ahead of all those other "frogs still sitting on logs!"

Making partnerships work is not magic – it just looks like it sometimes. Partnerships are all about people and, like everything else in business, and in life, they take thought, planning, hard work, determination, empathy, persistence, communication, and trust. When this is done right, it just looks like magic, and it pays off in a big way. Now go to it!

Notes

1. DDI's Trust: Strengthening the Foundation.
2. *The American Heritage® Dictionary of the English Language, Third Edition* copyright © 1992 by Houghton Mifflin Company. Electronic version licensed from INSO Corporation. All rights reserved.
3. Ibid.
4. Ibid.
5. Ibid.
6. Development Dimensions International "Partnerships: Creating Synergy."
7. Fandray, Dayton (2001) "Managing partnerships." *Continental*, May.
8. Kaydos, Will (1991) The Decision Group, author of *Measuring, Managing, and Maximizing Performance*. Productivity Press, Cambridge, MA; and (1999) *Operational Performance Measurement*. St Lucie Press, Boca Raton, FL.

Frequently Asked Questions (FAQs)

Q1: I have heard so many interchangeable uses of the terms partnerships and alliances. Are they really the same thing, or if they are different, how are they different?

A: See Chapter 2 Definition of Terms.

Q2: Why should I go to the trouble of forming partnerships anyway? Why not just go it alone?

A: See Chapter 1 Introduction and Categories of partnerships in Chapter 2 Definition of Terms.

Q3: What are the types of partnerships I might want to consider and why?

A: See Types and Categories of partnerships in Chapter 2 Definition of Terms and Chapter 5 The Global Dimension.

Q4: What are these new acronyms all about – CRM, DRM, CPFR – and what do they have to do with partnerships?

A: See Chapter 2 Definition of Terms.

Q5: Aren't partnerships and teams and collaboration all the same thing?

A: See Collaboration in Chapter 6 State of the Art.

Q6: What is a good example of a partnership in today's crazy business world?

A: See Southwest Airlines in Chapter 3 Evolution and several examples Chapter 6 State of the Art and Chapter 7 In Practice for leading examples.

Q7: What has happened to partnerships in the e-commerce world? Are they still viable?

A: See Chapter 4 The E-Dimension.

Q8: Does globalization really make much difference – aren't the principles of partnerships about the same all over?

A: See Chapter 5 The Global Dimension.

Q9: Partnerships are so "soft," how can they ever make it through tough times? Can you be part of a partnership and still have hard-nosed negotiations about issues like price, terms, etc.?

A: See Chapter 10 Ten Steps to Making it Work.

Q10: What will kill a partnership faster than ever, or make sure it'll never work in the first place?

A: See Chapter 10 Ten Steps to Making it Work and When information technology doesn't work ... in Chapter 7 In Practice.

Index

3Rs (risks, rewards, and resources) 124
accounting 45, 50-51
acquisitions 7, 17-18
airlines case study 77-8
alliances 7-8, 28-9, 47, 60-66, 77-8, 94-6
Amazon.com 29, 30-31
America Online (AOL) case study 21, 29, 85-7
Amrep case study 74-7
APS case study 80-83
Ariba case study 87-8
Assessment of Partnership Success 96-8

behavior 67-8
Bierce, Ambrose 16
books 112-15
Booz-Allen & Hamilton 8, 112
BP Amoco plc case study 84-5
Brewer, Peter 104-5
business (team) partner meeting 63

Canon case study 78-80
Carnegie, Andrew 17
case studies
   airlines 77-8
   America Online 85-7
   Amrep 74-7
   APS 80-83
   Ariba 87-8
   BP Amoco plc 84-5
   Canon 78-80
   Children's Hospital 57-8
   Cisneros Group of Companies (CGC) 83-4
   ConferenceDirect 54-7
   Dell 58-60
   Navistar 80-83
   Sony 85-7
CGC *see* Cisneros Group of Companies
champions 124-5
Chesbrough, Henry 33
chief executive officers (CEOs) 61, 62, 83-4
Children's Hospital case study 57-8
China 84-5
CHIPS (character, honesty, integrity, and principles) 120-122
Chrysler Corporation 3, 20-21
Cisneros Group of Companies (CGC) case study 83-4

coalitions, value networks 45
Coca-Cola 19
collaboration 65-6, 67-8, 99
Collaborative Planning, Forecasting, and Requirements (CPFR) 32, 36, 98-9
collective knowledge 67
Colvin, Geoffrey 34
commitment 124-5, 127
competitors 35
concepts 91-106
ConferenceDirect case study 54-7
consultants 112
cooperation 66
core competency 105
Covey, Stephen 121
Covisint 35-6, 37
CPFR see Collaborative Planning, Forecasting, and Requirements
CRM see Customer Relationship Management
culture 50-51, 85
Customer Relationship Management (CRM) 8-9, 35, 99-102
customers 6, 8-9, 98-102, 64, 44

Daimler-Benz 3, 17
DaimlerChrysler 20-21, 36, 37
Daly, James 94
databases 102-4
decision making 71
definitions 6-10
Dell case study 3, 58-60, 103
Dent, Stephen M. 66, 68-70, 92, 101, 113
DePree, Max 67
Disney 31, 83
Doz, Yves 41, 60
Drucker, Peter 3, 40, 49, 114-15
dynamic resource management (DRM) 102-4

e-commerce 9, 21-2, 27-37, 101
economy 45-6, 70-71
education 71
Electronic Data Interchange (EDI) 36
employees 6, 34-5, 44
environment 45-6
evolution 13-25
exchanges 35-7
executive meetings 62, 75

fit 122
Ford 2, 17, 20, 36, 37
franchises 56-7
frequently asked questions (FAQs) 129-30
Friedman, Thomas 23, 40, 41, 44, 46, 77, 115
functional partner meeting 63-4

Gallagher, Kevin 74-5, 76
Gartner Group 32, 34-5
gay rights 23-4
General Motors 2, 20, 36, 37
globalization 22-3, 50-51, 77, 79, 84-5, 39-51
goals 123
government 22-3, 45-6, 50-51
Graham, Mark 84-5
Greenhalgh, Leonard 57

Hamel, Gary 40, 41, 44, 45, 60, 113-14
Hansen, Morten 33
Hay, John 16
health care case study 57-8
Henkel 48-50, 85
history 13-25
Hunter, Dick 59, 60

i2 35, 59, 87-8
IBM 35, 88

independent contractor model 56-7
information
  computer programs 33-4
  CPFR 99
  filtered input 80-83
  new economics 42
  value networks 43-4
information technology 87-9
initiation 60-66
Internet 21-2, 27-37, 99-104, 41
iPlanet 35
irritants 63-5

Japan 20, 119
joint ventures 7, 84-5

Kaku, Ryuzaboro 78-9
Katzenbach, Jon 98
Kaydos, Will 104
keiretsu 20
key aspects
  concepts 91-106
  frequently asked questions 129-30
  resources 109-15
  ten steps 117-28
  thinkers 92-107
knowledge 43-4, 47, 67
Kyosei concept 78

LaLonde, Bud 70
leaders 46-7
Lean Production 20, 58
legal partnerships 8, 92-4, 112-13
Lewis, Jordan D. 7-8, 20, 54, 96, 112, 114
liabilities 92, 93, 94
limited partnerships 93

McDonald's 19
McGregor, Douglas 67, 113
Manco 48-50, 85, 99, 103

marketing 7, 9, 100
marketplaces 35-7
Maslow, Abraham 67-8, 69
measurement 104-5, 125-6
meetings 62-5, 75
mergers 7, 17-18
Michaels, James W. 59, 65, 83
Morgan, J.P. 17
Mott, Randy 58-9, 60
multi-level partnerships 61-2

Nasser, Jac 21
Navistar case study 80-83
networked incubators 32-3
networks *see* value networks
new economics 42
Nohria, Nitin 33

operational execution 42-3
oral agreements 93-4
outsourcing 10, 105-6

Partner Relationship Management (PRM) 8-9, 99-102
partners
  choice of 118, 126
  definition 14
  value networks 45
Partners Task Force (PTF) 23
"partnership," definition 6, 7, 14, 92
partnership agreement, definition 10
partnership meetings 62-5, 75
periodicals 110-11
Peters, Tom 114
power, history 16
PRM *see* Partner Relationship Management
Procter & Gamble 17, 33-4, 103
production, DRM 102-3
Prokopets, Len 65

quality management 68-70
Quinn, James Brian 105

recession 70-71
resources 109-15
rewards 124
risks 92, 93, 124
Rosen, Robert 9, 42, 50

sales automation, CRM 100
Schifrin, Matthew 4, 22, 25, 37
SCORE program 20-21
Sears 21
Shewhart PDCA process 68-70
Singapore 47
skills 7
Smith, Douglas 98
society, value networks 45-6
software 100, 102-4
Sony case study 85-7
Southwest Airlines 34-5
special partners 6
Speh, Tom 104-5
Star Alliance 77-8
Stengel, Casey 66
Stolle, Bryan 65
strategic alliances 6, 8, 57, 82-3, 94-6
strategic outsourcing 10, 105-6
Sull, Donald 33
suppliers 3, 6
  case studies 74-7
  CPFR 98-9
  CRM 101
  Dell 59-60
  exchanges and marketplaces 35-7
  giant corporations 19-21
  information technology 88-9
  irritants 64-5
  value networks 44, 45
supply-chain management 35, 44, 58-60
synergy 43-4, 86

technology 6, 7
thinkers 92-107
Time Warner 21, 29
time zones 62
Toyota 3, 20, 58
Toys "R" Us 30-31
transactional partnerships 7
Transora 35-7
Truax, Mitchell 57-8
trust 3, 21, 75, 87, 99, 103, 119-20

Uhlhorn, Martha 36
Uniform Partnership Act (US) 93
United Nations 18
United States of America
  history 15-16
  national allies 22-3
  Uniform Partnership Act 93

value networks 39-51
Vendor Appreciation Day 74-5
vertical integration 2
vice presidents (VPs) 61, 62, 63
Voluntary Inter-industry Commerce Standards (VICS) 98

Wal-Mart 21, 36-7, 48-50, 98-9, 103
Walton, Sam 113
Warner-Lambert 98-9, 103
Websites 110-11, 113
Woolgar, Steve 28, 29
World Wide Web 21-2